Praise For

MARRIAGES IN THE BIBLE

Every couple needs to read this book.

I've read hundreds of books on marriage, and this is one of the most memorable.

Dr Gary Lovejoy reminds us that there is so much to learn from the examples of others. With the wisdom of a Bible student, the curiosity of a college professor, and the compassion of a professional counselor the author guides us through many of the most common challenges that face marriages.

Rarely does a book entertain, teach, and challenge. This is such a book. Read it alone, read it with your spouse, read it with a group of other couples! Any way you read it, it will stretch you to make your marriage everything God wants it to be — a marriage where you love, protect, honor, forgive, sacrifice for, and enjoy your spouse.

Dr Lovejoy doesn't provide easy or simple steps to a happy marriage. He does something much better. He shows us time-tested principles from 17 real couples in the Bible. He brings these couples to life in such a vivid and practical way that we realize the struggles couples had thousands of years ago are no different than those we face today. From their examples we learn how to rise above our struggles to a place where God's love and grace can truly shine through us.

This book is not just about marriage, it's about being faithful follower of the one who made marriage. It's about being the best and most healthy person you can be.

Thank you, Dr Lovejoy, for showing us how relevant and practical God's Word is in the midst of this world's hardest challenges.

—Steve Stephens, PhD, Happy Valley, OR
President of EveryMarriageMatters and author of *Marriage:*
Experience the Best; 20 Rules and Tools for a Great Marriage;
Blueprints for a Solid Marriage; Lost in Translation.

***

Dr. Lovejoy has masterfully used his deep knowledge of human nature, historical texts, and ancient cultural insights to add rich texture to the marriages we see in the Bible. He skillfully brings out timeless principles from these marriages to apply to our marriages today. With the lessons learned from the good marriages, as well as the bad, Dr. Lovejoy empowers couples to strengthen and build-up their marriages to create loving, caring, happy relationships that can go the distance.

—Jennifer Streger Estrada,
CF APMP, Senior Proposal Writer, Eugene, OR for
Houghton Mifflin Harcourt Publishing Co.

***

"Protecting your marriage from the assault on its integrity and loyalty is paramount to preserving it," says Dr. Gary Lovejoy. At no other time in history have marriages been redefined, misunderstood, degraded, maligned, abandoned, and put to the test. In many cases, they fail – even those in the Bible. While we all want happy and fulfilling marriages, many of us don't know how to go about it. Happiness, it seems, is a byproduct of putting your spouse above yourself. This practice is often ridiculed by those who elevate self-interest above sacrifice. As Dr. Lovejoy reminds us, "The unexamined life is simply not an option if you want a satisfying marriage."

As a publicist, I have read *many dozens* of marriage books. This is the best! If you are serious about creating a marriage that thrives, I encourage you to read this book. If you know someone who is struggling, read this book. As he reminds us, "Marriage is a commitment borne on the wings of a love that embraces the whole person, warts and all."

—Don S. Otis
Veritas Communications, Sandpoint, ID
Author of *Whisker Rubs: Developing the Masculine Identity*

***

Insightful! Dr Lovejoy does a wonderful job of illuminating the strengths and weaknesses of marriages in a fallen world. His therapeutic insights are on full display as he walks through the marriages recorded in the Scriptures. This is truly a Romans 15:4 book: "For whatever was written in earlier times was written for our instruction so that through perseverance and the encouragement of the Scriptures we might have hope" (Romans 15:4). *Marriages in the Bible* is a must read as it helps to illuminate God's design for relationship in the midst of a broken world.

—Paul Govert, PsyD, Portland, OR
Private Practice Psychologist

***

Marriages in the Bible: What Do They Tell Us is an outstanding, applicable book for any couple who wants their marriage to grow stronger, healthier, and more loving. From the Bible, Dr. Lovejoy has skillfully unwrapped marriages and described aspects of their relationships that were both healthy and unhealthy. It is comforting to realize that Bible marriages had their difficulties too! However, it doesn't stop there. He then brings hope through the solid insight he deftly weaves into each story. He clearly shares key attributes that bring more love, joy and fulfillment to any marriage. His wisdom gleaned from the biblical overview becomes practical and applicable resources for us to utilize today.

We highly recommend this book! This book is an excellent resource for pastors and counselors to have in their offices ready to hand to any couple seeking more encouragement in their relationship.

—John and Marty Webb, McKinney, Texas
TriageCare Ministry

***

You know you have found a compelling, must-read book when the opening pages speak directly to you... which was my experience with THIS book. There are many books on biblical marriage, godly marriage principles, tools for Christian husbands and wives... but how many books truly take a deeper look at the actual couples and marriages in the Bible? Could it be that these Biblical examples of broken marriages, dysfunctional marriages, vibrant marriages, and enduring marriages are in and of themselves a wealth of practical, relevant, time-tested wisdom for us to glean from? The answer is an unqualified "YES!" Both my life and my marriage were richly blessed and deepened by this book—I'm confident yours will be too. Thank you, Dr. Lovejoy!

—Jay Messenger, Gresham, Oregon
Lead Pastor, Grace Community Church

Marriages in the Bible

What do they tell us?

by

Gary H. Lovejoy, Ph.D.

Acknowledgements

I wish to dedicate this book to the people who, over the years, have endeared themselves to me in ways that can only be described as transformative. Their deep and abiding love, their tender mercies in accepting my faults, and their intellectually provocative insights into Scripture have kept me true to God's Word.

I have had the distinct privilege of gathering with these uniquely gifted individuals on a bi-weekly basis for nearly 40 years; ours is a group which has committed itself to honoring God, honoring His Word, and honoring one another. They have been to me what the Inklings were to C.S. Lewis, but with the soft and loving touch of devoted wives thrown in for good measure. The Inklings were a literary discussion group composed of twelve regular members at the University of Oxford, who met weekly in town at the Eagle and Child Pub. In time, they became quite close to one another, especially men like J.R.R. Tolkien, C.S. Lewis and his brother Warren, Charles Williams, and Owen Barfield. It was, however, a men-only gathering. Unlike the Inklings, our wives have participated equally week after week in spiritually stimulating discussion which has added immeasurably to our mutual growth in knowledge of the Scriptures.

Calling ourselves a "Covenant Group" we have been ardently single-minded in our purpose to love, serve, pray for one another, and to build one another up in the Lord in the sweet fellowship of His grace and mercy.

These remarkable fellow travelers on the road to God's eternal rest, who emulate the Bible's most trusted ministers of divine purpose, are as follows:

Bill Mullins, a clinical psychologist, gifted with great knowledge and wisdom, but with the common touch, and with superior leadership ability added in for the bargain—he's the <u>Solomon</u> of our group;

Marlene Mullins, Bill's wife, an elementary school teacher, gifted with an amazingly tender heart for others, which leads to sacrificial service to both family and friends—she's the <u>Ruth </u>of our group;

Gregory Knopf, a family physician, intellectually gifted with an uncanny ability to ask the right questions (a good ability for a physician!) and the competence to take charge and get things done—he's the <u>Apostle Paul</u> of our group;

Bonnie Knopf, Greg's talented musician wife, gifted with a heart as big as all outdoors and an unparalleled ability to make good things happen, even under sorrowful conditions—she's the <u>Mary Magdalene</u> of our group who came from a tough beginning to become one of Jesus' most trusted and sociable followers;

Jeff Nelson, a business man, gifted with a lovable heart of great honesty and humility (in him is no guile) and a relentless commitment to serve God—he's the <u>Apostle Nathaniel</u> (John 1: 47) of our group;

Maren Nelson, Jeff's wife, another elementary school teacher, gifted with a sweet attitude of self-sacrifice and a Christ-like desire help others in desperate need—she's the <u>Mary, sister of Martha</u>, of our group, one who eagerly listens to Jesus in her life;

Sue Lovejoy, my precious wife, a former teacher and subsequently a highly respected general office manager, gifted with an impressive combination of a keen business mind with a quiet, but unwavering devotion to putting her faith into action—she's the <u>Lydia</u> of our group, an example of a respected businesswoman who is an unassuming, faithful disciple beloved by God and by all who know her.

Together these incomparable companions of Christian fellowship have left nothing less than a permanent imprint on my life and work.

Contents

Preface

Almost everyone who enters into marriage does so with the highest hopes and the belief that it will provide the intimacy and companionship they so dearly desire. Their breathless romance is usually running high, their patience waiting for the "big day" is running low, and their optimism for the future is off the scale. They can't even imagine that anything could go wrong. They are convinced their love for one another will carry them through whatever adversity they might face. The idea that they might become disillusioned down the road doesn't even occur to them.

It happens, and with greater regularity than you might expect. Marriage is a complex union, with many moving parts. Once the marriage starts showing cracks at the seams, things often begin to move very quickly. It's usually the wife who initially sounds the alarm. The husband, feeling an increasing sense of panic inside, often buries the problems, hoping if he looks the other way they'll somehow magically go away on their own. Of course, that never works.

Both spouses are often at a loss about how to stem the growing tide of dissatisfaction. To their credit, they may dig into self-help books on marriage, or consult psychologists, pastors, marriage counselors, or other relationship experts. They may even attend marriage seminars, always looking for the right formula for a happy marriage. They often learn some valuable principles along the way, but there remains the angst that something is still missing.

Most sermons on marriage direct your attention to well-worn passages like Paul's letter to the Ephesians or his admonitions to the Corinthians or to Jesus' own teachings on marriage in the Gospels. Such sermons are useful for reminding us of the core teachings on marriage in the Bible, but the lights fail to go on for many with regard to what these principles look like in action. Couples may have lots of raw knowledge at their disposal but lack the models to make it stick when applying it to their own relationships.

The perspective of this book is that because we rarely, if ever, examine the dynamics of marriages in the Bible, whether good or bad, how can we possibly know what their strengths and weaknesses are? In our obsession with principles, we've paid scant attention to the many examples God has given us to help us understand how they truthfully work and what happens when they're ignored or rejected.

To make up for this deficit, this book carefully explores seventeen marriages in the Old and New Testaments to see what they can tell us about what we can do and what we should avoid doing in building marriages that last. Surprisingly, these scriptural relationships, even the severely dysfunctional ones, offer a wealth of understanding to the couple who is genuinely interested in "divorce proofing" their marriage. This includes engaged couples planning to marry, newly married couples, and those with varied lengths of marriage wanting to improve their relationships.

It's my hope that this will become the enlightening journey you've been looking for which joins principles and pragmatism, concepts and function.

Part one - The Humility of Happiness

Chapter 1

Confronting What We Fear and Why

A secular author once said "…a perfect marriage is just two imperfect people who refuse to give up on each other."[1] That may be true for some marriages that seem to last beyond others' expectations, but long-term marriages aren't necessarily happy ones. If the aim is to have a *fulfilling marriage,* it starts with recognizing your own imperfections first, then forgiving those of your partner.

The key challenge to reaching that goal is to recognize those imperfections in yourself without lapsing into self-loathing. That's important; ironically, self-hatred is the most common reason a person fails to forgive the wrongs of others. At first, that may seem counter-intuitive, but self-hatred (frequently called, "low self-esteem") highly sensitizes you to any perceived slight, real or imaginary. What's more, it constantly informs you to remain on high alert for others' attempts to victimize you. It's no surprise to find that such sensitivity predisposes a spouse to overreact to nearly every misstep in a marriage.

As it turns out, the capacity to admit to your own wrongs and forgive yourself is just as important as addressing and forgiving your partner's wrongs. Instead of becoming defensive and lashing out at your partner, if you acknowledge the possibility that you might have misread the situation or reacted to it poorly, you may very well discover the miraculous power of

---

[1] Kate Stewart, "Loving the White Liar", CreateSpace Independent Publishing Platform, 2015, p. 72

humility to restore calm. Doing this — not in a groveling, self-effacing or even manipulative way but in an assertive, proactive way — is essential to the creation of a level playing field emotionally.

So asking for forgiveness is just as important, if not more important a part of this process as providing it, if you want to reduce the toxicity of your interactions. Some avoid doing that because they fear that it would make them appear weak or would be tantamount to admitting their complicity in the relational misfire. To them, it's important never to give ground, never to confess to personal wrongs. While it may be hard to acknowledge, it takes a humble spirit to open the door to reconciliation. It must involve a conversation, not about who's right and who's wrong but about what can change in your marriage to make things better.

We can usually find imperfections quite easily in our partners. In fact, it's frequently the only thing we can see. People are remarkably prone to mutter to themselves, "He's so stubborn," or "She's being so unreasonable," without considering how they are coming across. This typically ignites an internal narrative about how unhappy they are and how victimized by their spouses they feel, an internal narrative which inevitably leads to further conflict and anger. That's why marriage is a common ground for self-fulfilling prophecies, perhaps more than almost any other relationship we have.

But there's the rub. We are often quite convinced that our perception of the interaction is the correct one and that our partner's recollection is simply flawed. Recently, I saw a young woman wearing a T-shirt that read, "I'm not arguing; I'm just explaining why I'm right!" That amusing aphorism pretty much captures it.

Many arguments consist mostly of trying to "explain" to your insensitive and bull-headed partner what *really* happened and why he or she is in the wrong. It's what we call the "self-summarizing syndrome" because you find yourself constantly repeating the same lines over and over, as if repeating them will magically make it true, or at least convince your spouse to back down. Unfortunately, no one wins at this game.

That's because these arguments are mainly attempts to first accuse your partner of callous disregard of the "facts", forcing them to defend themselves, and, second. to convince him or her that you are the victim of an unfair attack. It boils down to reinforcing a narrative of helplessness that breeds its own kind of resentment; that only further deepens the divide. Since you end up believing it's entirely your partner's fault, then it's up to him or her –not you – to fix it. Do you see how easy it is to disown responsibility to work on your marriage and instead to descend into despair about it?

Once you have handed over the reins of positive change to your spouse, you have forfeited your chances to make a difference in your marriage. You then cease to be a proactive force for growth in your relationship. Instead, you become a passive, though sullen, spectator to its demise. You also become chronically frustrated that your marriage doesn't make you happy, not realizing that *you* are the one who can make it happy for you.

Leo Tolstoy (1828-1910), the great Russian author, once observed that "…what counts in making a happy marriage is not so much how compatible you are, but how you deal with incompatibility."[2] Although you may have been attracted to your spouse because of what you had in common, it's the differences that force you out of the pocket to grow as a person.

Too many people try to subdue their differences in the name of accommodation rather than to creatively deal with them in the open. If you succeed in becoming clones of one another, genuine interest in the relationship is the primary casualty. No one remains interested in someone for long if that person is merely a mirror image of their own thoughts and feelings. The relationship then suffers from massive redundancy, resulting in suffocating inertia. They become bored with the marriage. No negotiations are necessary. No one is pushed out of their comfort zone. Growth is at a virtual standstill. The life of the relationship slowly withers and dies.

Whether you keep your thoughts and feelings to yourself or you belligerently force them on your partner, it's usually because you're fearful that otherwise your partner will reject them. Perhaps you were taught early in life not to expect to be listened to or accepted for who you are or for what you think. Maybe you saw other family members getting squashed if they expressed their dissent or ignored if they tried to express their points of view. You learned that revealing your insides was a dangerous business and therefore best to avoid at all costs.

Both aggression and passivity achieve the avoidance a person seeks. One intimidates into submission so that there's no need to discuss differences; the other internalizes everything, thus keeping whatever differences that exist a mutually agreed upon secret.

---

[2] Leo Tolstoy, personal quote, reproduced on Goodreads.com, October, 2022

Both are a cover for fear — the fear of conflict, which exposes your feelings of inferiority or inadequacy, or the fear of intimacy, which only increases the emotional stakes, or maybe even the fear of differentness itself. Whatever the reason, transparency is sacrificed on the altar of emotional safety.

Fear of your spouse's reactions does not lead to interpersonal cowardice without a background that created it. You may have been taught to fear others' responses that are different than yours because you've been conditioned to think that the fear reflects your unworthiness to be heard. Any perceived difference is seen as an assault on your personhood, an attack on the value of your ideas. It's impossible to express true humility without the self-esteem that comes from knowing someone else cannot invalidate your thoughts and feelings.

Self-esteem or, as some prefer, self-respect, is not an over-inflated sense of self or egotism gone rogue. Nor does it have anything to do with the biblical injunction against "thinking of yourself more highly than you ought" (Rom. 12:3). The Apostle Paul used that phrase to refer to the idea that some, like the Pharisees, wrongly assumed a kind of spiritual superiority over others.

As contradictory as it may seem, attitudes of superiority are usually the product of *low* self-esteem, not the other way around. Assuming a posture of superiority is intuitively designed to elicit the envy and/or admiration of others to counter the worthlessness you would otherwise feel inside if you stopped denying it to yourself.

The dominant concern is with what other people will think of you. In effect, you create a false equivalency between your worth and other people's evaluations of you. You end up constantly seeking the approval of others without letting on that you need their admiration to prop you up emotionally.

Low self-esteem turns your attention inward, desperately seeking any kind of affirmation, even if that means the pretense of self-aggrandizement; you're bracing for disapproval all the time. As a counterweight to deeper feelings of inferiority, you become hypervigilant to any clues that your credibility might be challenged. You'll do anything to avoid coming across as a fool or looking like "an idiot", even though you may feel that way inside. Or, you might aggressively take dictatorial command of the situation — become a bully of sorts — blunting any criticism whatsoever. Those who take this approach often become paranoid about the slightest indication of dissent.

The most dramatic historical example of this phenomenon is seen in the rise of Adolf Hitler. Because he was a rejected artist who had been given the thumbs down by the elite international art community in Vienna, his inferiority feelings had exploded into self-hatred and profound depression. That's when he turned his attention to the angry world of post World War I German politics, becoming obsessed with promoting the superiority of the Aryan race, of which he was a part. Scapegoating the Jews gave him the excuse to be the one doing the rejecting rather than being the one who was rejected. The results were, of course, as tragic as they were extreme.

In contrast, humility turns your attention outward, toward serving the needs of others. It requires a healthy self-concept that accepts who you are as one of God's beloved children. It's based on a sense of self-worth affirmed in Christ and a sense of adequacy empowered by the Holy Spirit. You don't need to seek the approval of others to feel worthwhile or demand attention from others in order to feel significant because you already have those in your relationship with God. You are free to look outward, actively listen to others and to respond without demanding what's in it for you.

When Jesus confronted His disciples over their arguments about who will be the greatest in heaven, He told them He identified with the servant, not the master of the house. That answer came only after they had fingered the master of the house as greater than his servant. Then He revealed that the greatest in the kingdom of God is the one who humbly serves. It's unlikely they ever forgot that lesson!

Humility is not self-abnegation or self-hatred. In fact, it's quite the opposite since you are no longer laboring to establish your worth. Most of the obnoxious behaviors people engage in are connected in some way to trying to prove their significance to others. Whether they're constantly bragging about their latest accomplishments or busy throwing their weight around to impress or frighten you, they're essentially broadcasting their own insecurity about who they are.

Neither is humility telling others how inadequate or worthless you are or acting in self-deprecating ways. The righteous life is not a contest to see how far you can go to lower yourself in the eyes of others. That may be a good strategy for eliciting pity from others, but it's a poor advertisement for a life in Christ. If you believe God created you, do you really think He wants you to spend your days devaluing what He has created? God forbid.

When Jesus talked about humility in terms of serving others, He was talking about the winsomeness of true piety, unlike that false piety of the Pharisees. He taught about the importance of denying self, by which He meant denying selfish desires, not about self-denial, which is merely another name for the self-imposed deprivation of legalistic restrictions. Seeking the attention or approval of others is not denying self. Neither is soliciting their pity. And it certainly isn't the over spiritualized lectures of the self-righteous. Instead, focusing on what God lovingly thinks of you is what's at the heart of Jesus' teaching, because, frankly, it's the only view that prompts you to love others without a hidden agenda.

In the Apostle John's first letter, he speaks of perfect love casting out fear. He described himself as the "beloved disciple of Jesus", not because he was trying to pump up his resume or claim that he was more special than the other disciples, but because it was Jesus' love for him that had transformed his life. Though he comes across as an even-tempered member of Jesus' inner circle, Jesus called John and his brother James the "sons of thunder", suggesting they could become volatile at times.

Jesus likely knew John and his brother before He called them, since they were part of his extended family. They were, in fact, his cousins, as their mother, Salome, was the sister of Jesus' mother (Matthew 27: 56; Mark 15: 40). He may have even known what they were like as fishermen on the Sea of Galilee, which could have given rise to the metaphoric description He gave them.

In any case, it's not the picture most people have of John. Instead, he's typically seen as more serene and unflappable, in contrast to Peter, who is depicted as full of bluster. Perhaps it was his experience of Jesus' deep, unconditional love, together with His aura of personal peace, which had a pronounced calming effect on John. Certainly, that's what seeps through the pages of Scripture. It's not surprising that it was John who called out the fact that the remedy for fear, and the behaviors that flow from it, is God's love (1 John 4: 18). If love casts out fear, especially the fear of one's eternal destiny, then the inevitable result is personal peace. It follows that love should cast out self-hatred as well, since it's usually at the base of that fear.

Jesus taught the downtrodden and those who were treated as outcasts of Jewish society that God valued them, that they were precious in His sight. He wanted them to see themselves through the eyes of God, which was very different than the way the culture treated them. In realizing their true value to God, Jesus knew it would transform their view of themselves and would turn their full attention to the good news He had to share. He was, after all, seeking redemption for both their minds and their souls.

All the factors we've discussed so far are important to consider when we examine what determines the differences between a happy marriage and an unhappy one. Every relationship has its unique issues, but there are identifiable patterns that predict the most likely outcomes in the struggle to make a good life together.

The Bible is filled with examples of both good marriages and bad, which give us glimpses of how God viewed them. Some involve characters you are very familiar with, but others are more obscure. Regardless of whether they are high profile or not, they each provide valuable lessons we can apply to our own marriages. So, let's take a look at some of them and see what we can learn.

Part Two - Patriarchal Marriages

Chapter 2

Abraham and Sarah: Where's My Man When I Need Him?
Genesis 12: 1-20; 16:1-15; 20:1-17; 21:1-13

The Bible doesn't discuss the courtship of Abraham and Sarah, but it's not difficult to figure out how they first knew each other. We learn this from one of Abraham's morally questionable rationales which he used for asking his wife to assume an identity that would protect his own life. It turns out that Sarah's pretense in posing as Abraham's sister was only a half truth. Abraham justified his request of Sarah by resorting to the fact that she was after all his half-sister. They had the same father but different mothers.

Marriages among siblings or other close family members were more common in the early days of civilization when the world population was still relatively sparse and opportunities to find a mate were limited. Beginning with the sons and daughters of Adam and Eve, who had no choice but to marry their siblings and close relatives, these conditions continued through to well after the Flood, when the grandchildren of Noah had to intermarry among their cousins.

Besides, at the time, it was unlikely that the genetic pool had been significantly contaminated, as became the case later on when marrying siblings or other close relatives was prohibited. What's more, there is no evidence that Abraham had violated any law, since the incest laws introduced by Moses weren't established until some 500 years after Abraham. He could hardly have been held responsible for laws (e.g., Deut. 27:22) that God had yet to reveal.

By the time of Moses, the risk of genetic defects was great enough that close intermarriages were no longer safe. God's intent has always been to protect His people, which also is the reason for many of the hygiene and dietary laws in the book of Leviticus.

To Abraham's shame as a husband, however, he forced Sarah to deliberately lie about their relationship by resorting to a half truth, not once but twice (first with the Egyptian Pharaoh and, then with King Abimelech), to save his own skin. In the Ancient Near East, adultery was considered a serious crime, which is why, once Abimelech discovered the truth about Sarah, he, like Pharaoh, was angry with Abraham. Accordingly, he ordered his men not to touch Sarah or else they would be put to death. Kings in that day exclusively took virgins into their harems and appointed castrated eunuchs (who posed no threat to their virginity) as administrators over them. Abraham had likely reasoned that, if the Philistines believed Sarah was his wife, they might kill him, thereby claiming her to be a widow and thus eligible to be remarried. In that case one of them could have her for himself without concern for legal reprisal.

Nonetheless, for Abraham to put his own wife at risk of violating their marital covenant was unconscionable. Not only was it a selfish act on his part, but it also failed to demonstrate a love that was worthy of his marriage. Regrettably, fear can lead to a variety of dishonest behaviors which can be quite damaging to a relationship.

No mention is made in the descriptions of these episodes of exactly how Sarah was feeling about what Abraham was asking her to do. But it's not a stretch of the imagination to believe that she was deeply hurt by his selfish demands. As a dutiful wife, she apparently thought she had no other recourse but to go along with the ruse. After all, women in ancient Jewish society were considered little more than the personal property of men, and had little say in what happened to them.

Nevertheless, the trust levels in their marriage were irreparably harmed. If she was that vulnerable to being shipped off to some stranger her husband was afraid of, what confidence would she have that it wouldn't happen again? Perhaps the hormonal condition of her barrenness was exacerbated by the enormous emotional stress of being so expendable and never knowing if or when she would be dispatched to another feared enemy of her husband's. It would certainly be a hard way to live.

But Abraham's failure to be protective of his wife did not stop there. Later, when Sarah's Egyptian handmaiden Hagar became pregnant with Abraham's first child (following the ancient primary-secondary wife custom of providing an heir), Sarah had to endure Hagar's taunts about being an inadequate wife. This taunting apparently went on for some time before Sarah had enough and demanded Abraham do something about it.

He had to have known what was going on right under his nose, but had failed to take any action. In full avoidance mode, he had essentially ignored the situation, probably hoping it would resolve itself over time. His passivity deeply angered Sarah who had patiently waited for Abraham to intervene. When he didn't, she finally blew her top and, in a rare display of righteous indignation, confronted her husband:

> *"You are responsible for the wrong I am suffering. I put my servant in your arms, and now that she knows she's pregnant, she despises me. May the Lord judge between you and me"* (Gen. 6: 5).

There was always the potential for the primary-secondary wife custom to be disruptive, a custom in which a barren wife felt obligated to give her female servant to her husband to serve as a proxy or secondary wife to provide him an heir. It was essentially a culturally sanctioned sexual affair based on the rationale that, under certain conditions, the arrangement to bring in a "substitute wife" was necessary for the perpetuation of the family line.

This custom was often fraught with jealousies, disaffections, and prejudice, which soured the original relationship, as can be seen in Abraham and Sarah's marriage. The practice of having concubines for the same purpose began during the morally corrupt period of the infamous Nimrod's reign, so these sorts of arrangements originated in the darkened hearts of sinful men, not in the commands of a righteous God. By the time of Abraham, they were well-ingrained in the culture and this custom was never even questioned. That said, Abraham must have known what was going on inside his own tent, even though he had been derelict in his duty to stop it. His response to Sarah's outburst was quite telling. He said to her, "Your servant is in your hands. Do with her whatever you think best" (vs. 6). In other words, he was saying, "It's your problem, so you fix it." This was like

Pilate washing his hands at Jesus' trial and telling the Pharisees he didn't want anything to do with His conviction.

Sarah was begging Abraham to step up to the plate and do what was right. It was his responsibility as her husband to protect her from the verbal assaults of anyone. They both knew that Abraham, as the head of the household, could have given just one stern warning to Hagar, one which promised consequences if she didn't cease her taunting, and it would most likely have taken care of the problem.

But Abraham didn't want to get involved in the spat between the two women. It's likely he hated interpersonal conflict, so when it occurred, he ran for the hills. Intervening between two angry women was not his idea of a desirable encounter. Instead, he washed his hands of the whole matter, leaving it to Sarah to take action, which was the final straw for her. Of course, in her state of outrage — outrage at Hagar for her taunts and at Abraham for not going to bat for her — she was bound to handle the problem poorly.

Sarah began wrongly abusing Hagar so much that she ran away to salvage what remained of her emotional sanity. Ironically, as is so often the case where irresponsibility is the issue, it ended up causing Abraham far more headaches than if he had taken action in the first place. Avoidance is rarely the answer. Ultimately, he had to go after Hagar and bring her back, finally laying down some long overdue ground rules for their conduct with each other.

The persistent problem in their marriage was a husband who habitually failed to adequately protect his wife, either physically or emotionally, and a wife who either waited too long to call him on it, or was complicit in it because it was largely the product of cultural expectations, not because she was too timid to speak up as she did later.

One can only imagine how painful the whole matter was to her, given her repeated belief that God had cursed her with a barren womb. Hagar had simply piled on to her grief, adding even more reasons to feel useless and depressed. After all, in that day, the woman's primary role was seen as raising children for her husband's posterity.

There is no evidence that Abraham understood either the depth of her despair or her feelings of isolation as a wife displaced by her slave in the central role of providing children. He seemed too self-centered for that level of insight. Even if he did, he showed remarkably little empathy for Sarah. By ignoring her conflict with Hagar, he only deepened the emotional wounds she had so plainly suffered (Gen. 16:1-6; 21:8-13).

When it came to tenderness, Abraham appeared rather stoic, which may have been one reason there was no emotional response from him recorded when he was asked to sacrifice his son Isaac. He must have been deeply torn by what he was asked to do and enormously relieved when the angel of the Lord intervened and provided a ram caught in the thickets nearby for the sacrifice. But no mention is made of the possibility of God stopping the sacrifice of his son in his recorded interactions with Isaac, even when his son specifically asked where the sacrificial lamb was. Isaac had probably already begun to suspect that *he* was the sacrifice, since child sacrifice was not uncommon in those days. Even Sarah may have privately wondered the same thing as she watched them head off to the mountains with a load of wood in tow. He simply told Isaac that God would provide the lamb without revealing what God had said to him. Perhaps his confidence in the Lord's mercy rendered a more complete answer moot in his mind. In any case, he didn't waver in his belief that God would fulfill his promise of a nation of descendants through Isaac.

The whole experience had pitted his natural feelings as a father who loved his son against the command of God. There is some evidence he believed that God would, in the end, spare his son, even if it meant He would subsequently raise him up from the dead (Heb. 11: 19). Still, that would mean he would have sacrificed his son, witnessing his pain and agony in the process. It's what made child sacrifice particularly ugly (not to mention detestable to God).

On the other hand, it was stark testimony to the power of Abraham's faith in the goodness of his God. But the fact that the Bible is silent about any expressions of emotion on Abraham's part suggests that he apparently kept all his emotions to himself. He seems to have been, for the most part, an internalizer.

Sometimes, such silence occurs because people are too afraid to tell the truth. They comfort themselves with the mistaken notion that it's somehow more loving not to tell the other person what they're feeling or the truth about what's happening. But that's turning love into a kind of idolatry in which you sacrifice intimacy at the fearful behest of the imagined demand for secrecy.

Of course love is not about beating someone over the head with transparency. Neither is it avoiding conversation altogether. It's about truthful self-disclosure given with gentleness and kindness; it involves being tenderly assertive without being destructively aggressive.

To be fair to Abraham, we may not have been told what he was feeling simply because such information was secondary to the point being made about his remarkable obedience. His trust in the Lord was unparalleled, given what God was asking him to do, especially since he was unaware, up to that point, that child sacrifice was utterly loathsome to the One he worshipped.

Though his marriage to Sarah managed somehow to rise above these drawbacks, many a marriage is doomed, if not by an emotionally sterile relationship, then by such a reckless disregard for the emotional safety of the other person. Though Abraham was a man of unmatched faith, he was not without his faults that did, in fact, cause much grief to his wife. We must be honest: While he was obedient to God's commands, he was not always obedient to his responsibilities as a loving husband, which sometimes led to Sarah's angry outbursts (e.g., Gen. 16:1-6; 21:8-13). He seemed perpetually slow to acknowledge Sarah's travails, often failing to respond until Sarah had had a meltdown.

***

Points to Ponder

Today, the challenge to protect one's spouse more often surfaces when an over-controlling mother-in-law or father-in-law is constantly trying to manipulate the marriage of their son or daughter. Whether this is done indirectly by the cold shoulder treatment, or directly by making unreasonable demands on them, it's difficult to overestimate how destructive such interference can be to a marriage.

If the son or daughter whose parents are interfering refuses to side with their marriage partner in achieving independence, but, hangs that partner out to dry by caving in to every demand that his or her parents make, it often spells disaster. It creates a major divide in the relationship, often one that becomes irreparable.

Such symbiotic connections between parents and their adult children can destroy the sense of "togetherness" in a marriage, thereby loosening an important anchor in its stability. Protecting your marriage from the assaults on its integrity and loyalty is paramount to preserving it. That's true whether those assaults come from the attacks of others outside the extended family or from the pressures brought to bear by those within it.

When a wife, for example, no longer feels her husband will protect her from over-bearing family members such as the in-laws, or from disparaging remarks made by friends, she feels overwhelmingly alone and unloved. What's more, she comes to believe that she stands no chance of ever being heard. If, on the other hand, a husband feels he must always take a back seat to the influence of, say, his wife's mother in his marriage, he will not only come to despise his mother-in-law, but also his wife for always siding with her.

Spouses struggling with the issue of "inclusion" in their marriages, in which they feel like they're on the outside looking in, will naturally start to emotionally distance from those relationships. If the situation fails to change, then you can expect alienation, and then an eventual divorce. A marriage cannot usually withstand the specter of divided loyalties for long.

When someone you see often as a couple has a habit of saying unkind things to your spouse and you let it pass, hoping it will blow over or thinking that it's your spouse's responsibility, not yours, to handle, don't be surprised if you get blowback for your silence. If, for instance, your wife comes to you complaining about the treatment she is getting from someone, and you reply with something like, "Oh, you know Marcia, that's what's she's like; just let it roll off your back!" you're probably not going to like her response.

Anger is the common response you get when your spouse's concern is dismissed or she is asked to merely shrug it off. If a wife comes to her husband about such concerns, she expects, or at the very least, hopes, for protection from getting further abused by others. Sarah had waited too long to go to Abraham, as evident from the fact that she was angry before she even talked to him about her problem with Hagar's sarcastic insults. She, no doubt, had hoped he would have done something about it without her having to say anything. But his passivity had worn thin by the time she got around to confronting him (Gen. 21:8-10).

If you want your wife to feel she's important to you, then it's best to take some kind of action, even if it's simply taking her out of the situation with the promise that she won't have to be subjected to that again. Doing nothing is not really an option if you want a happy marriage.

By properly calling out the offensive comments (i.e., speaking the truth in love—Eph. 4:15) and asking the offender to stop making those remarks, you're telling your wife that you want to protect her. This can be done privately to avoid embarrassment to either party, but your spouse needs to know it happened. Regardless of what the other person does in response, you have sent a clear message that you love your wife and will always protect her whenever you can.

The fact that Abraham failed to do this rendered him a curiously paradoxical figure. In some areas of his life he was quite proactive, even courageous, such as leading his immediate family to strike off on their own to parts unknown at the behest of God's calling, or almost single-handedly saving his nephew, Lot, from enemies who had captured him. But in other areas, especially in domestic matters, he proved to be surprisingly hesitant and fearful, seemingly unable to confront problems directly. This becomes even more significant in cases where children are involved. Whether it concerns natural or adopted children, a father who avoids conflict can be problematic not only for child rearing but also for the tranquility of his marriage.

Though they obviously remained together, the marriage of Abraham and Sarah would have been a much happier one had this paradox not existed. It's true that they were on the same page spiritually, yet in the home there was a damaging division between them. Either by neglect or more likely by avoidance, they let issues drag on too long without any corrective action, something which clearly did their relationship no favors.

No marriage is designed to flourish without concerted efforts to address the concerns of one another.

You ignore them at your peril.

Chapter 3

Isaac and Rebekah: The Boomerang of Deception
Genesis 24L62-67; 25:19-26; 26:1-11; 27:1-28:9

In Genesis 26, we read that Isaac, Abraham's son, committed the same sin as his father; he pawned off his wife Rebekah as his sister. It proved the age-old adage, "the apple doesn't fall far from the tree."

In Isaac's case, however, he couldn't even legitimately claim that Rebekah was his half-sister, albeit she was a relative. Rebekah was the granddaughter of Abraham's brother Nahor and his wife Milcah (who was the daughter of Haran, Abraham's other brother). Technically, that made her Isaac's grandniece. Calling her his sister — the looser meaning of the term "sister" notwithstanding — was a bit of a stretch.

Nonetheless, he used the same rationale that his father had used and did so with the men who served the same King Abimelech of Gerar. Obviously, Abraham and his son had talked about these matters, a conversation which had apparently convinced Isaac that it was a good strategy to follow. Meanwhile, King Abimelech must have wondered what was wrong with this family. They probably seemed scared of their own shadows and incapable of telling the truth.

At least he could give them credit for thinking their wives were beautiful. In any case, King Abimelech roundly rebuked Isaac for deceiving him, which he interpreted as setting him up for a curse from God.

You have to wonder whether Isaac anticipated the possibility of being humiliated by the king, but decided to take the risk anyway because his fear was too great to do otherwise. He must have known that part of Abraham's story, but that was not enough to deter him from trying to deceive Abimelech and his men once again.

It seems that the failures of both Isaac and his father to protect their wives because of their greater interest in protecting themselves had become an endemic, cross-generational problem. It would have been, at minimum, interesting to listen in on some of the private conversations between Rebekah and her mother-in-law, Sarah; no doubt they must have commiserated about their husbands' apparent inability to stand up for them. Perhaps Rebekah took some solace in the fact that it wasn't something lacking in her that prompted her husband to engage in such cowardly duplicity, but was merely a less than admirable family trait.

As with Sarah, there is no indication that Rebekah ever discussed with Isaac what she felt about his willingness to give her away because he was afraid for his own life. In fact, there is no mention of what she felt about it at all. But this behavior couldn't be chalked up as merely another one of those cultural conventions that was demeaning to women. Giving your handmaiden to your husband so that she could have sex with him and hopefully sire a son couldn't have been an easy custom for any woman, though acceptance of it was expected if the woman didn't want to be condemned for denying her husband an heir.

This was different; this sprang from Isaac's own fear, no matter how real or imagined it may have been. It unfortunately implied that his life was more important than hers, which in that day was a common belief in society. Still it had to hurt Rebekah, coming as it did from her own husband.

As wrenching as this episode must have been, Isaac and Rebekah's problems didn't stop there. When the twins Jacob and Esau came along, a destructive divide began between the two of them over a dreadful parenting bias. As the boys grew up, each parent developed a favorite son with whom they became allied in the quest to secure the brightest possible promise of a prosperous future.

Esau, the oldest by a few minutes, was a brash, impulsive young man whose best talents were found in the field, where the rough and tumble adventure of hunting game required skill with a bow and arrow. Raw around the edges, he was a rugged man of the hills, an intrepid, even audacious, outdoorsman, whom Isaac seemed to favor as a "man's man". He even had a hairy appearance, fitting for a gruff, over-confident hunter who spent many a night sleeping on the ground. It is recorded that Isaac loved the taste of game, and it was Esau alone who supplied it for him.

Jacob, on the other hand, was a homebody who preferred domestic pursuits such as cooking, much to the delight of his mother Rebekah. He was quieter and more refined in temperament, but very clever and with a tendency to be deceptive when he wanted to be. Although he enjoyed household responsibilities, he always kept his eye on ways to take advantage of a situation for his own gain. His name, Jacob, which means in Hebrew, "to deceive", fit him quite well.

Although the eldest son Esau had foolishly given away his birthright (Gen 25:29-34) to Jacob in an impetuous moment of hunger coming in from a hunting trip, he still was in line to receive his father's blessing. Rebekah had other plans. She nefariously conspired with Jacob to receive that blessing as well before it could be given to Esau. It's doubtful that the two of them could have pulled it off without the aid of Isaac's blindness in old age.

After preparing a special dish of choice goat meat just the way she knew her husband liked it, Rebekah helped Jacob disguise his identity by slipping into one of Esau's tunics and covering the exposed parts of his body with goat skins to simulate Esau's hairy arms and neck. Because he was skeptical at first that Esau could return so quickly from his hunting trip, Isaac had asked Jacob to come closer so he could touch him to see if it was really his son, Esau. It was a very tense moment for Jacob, who had already questioned whether they could successfully fool his father.

Isaac's initial suspicions were probably heightened by his awareness that his wife preferred Jacob to receive the blessing. He probably didn't put it past her (or Jacob) to try and trick him. In the end, the ruse worked, with Isaac subsequently convinced that he was giving his blessing to Esau. When Esau discovered he'd been ripped off by his brother again, he threatened to kill Jacob as soon as his father died. This was a threat Rebekah treated seriously enough to swing into action. She sent Jacob to her brother Laban, who lived up north in Paddan Aram, safely out of Esau's clutches. Jacob lived there for the next twenty years.

The Bible doesn't describe Isaac's response to Rebekah once he found out he had been tricked into giving his blessing to Jacob, not Esau, but it was likely a very angry one. It may very well have created an emotional barrier between them that lasted the rest of their marriage, especially since it was a betrayal that couldn't be undone.

This is the collateral damage of an unhealthy favoritism in parenting, which pushes spouses to compete against each other for their favored child to end up with the best outcomes. As we can see, it profoundly affected the relationship between Jacob and Esau, creating a separation between them that lasted over two decades.

If God had confronted them about their problem, it wouldn't have been surprising to see Isaac and Rebekah also using Adam's approach to absolving themselves of culpability. If you recall, Adam had pointed his finger at Eve and declared she was the guilty party. When Eve heard this, deprived of her chance to blame Adam, she turned around and accused the serpent of deceiving her.

Admitting guilt has forever been a difficult thing for most people to do. That's why King David's unhesitant admission of guilt over the events around his affair with Bathsheba stands out in the Bible. It's a major reason God declared that David was a man after His own heart, despite the egregious nature of his sin.

It's doubtful, in any event, that either Isaac or Rebekah fully acknowledged their sin. They were too busy looking out for the interests of their favorite child to think that their actions were harming the family and especially their marriage. In the end, Isaac likely sulked in the agonizing reality that he had given his blessing to the wrong son, something he could never take back. Seething over his wife's (and Jacob's) betrayal would have begged the question of his own guilt of favoritism.

Meanwhile, Rebekah probably took comfort in knowing Jacob was set for life, even if it was at the expense of Esau. She may even have thought that the outcome was worth the damage she did to her marriage. After all, she could have reasoned that if she hadn't taken action, it would have been the rough-hewn Esau who was living the charmed life, leaving the more refined Jacob to eke out a living from the soil.

Contrary to whatever rationale she used, the subterranean power struggles between her and her husband actually left nothing but a trail of losers, all resentful toward one another to varying degrees. What's more, the damage was not confined to the immediate family; it extended to future generations as well.

You can see this tendency for dysfunctional parenting styles translating into intergenerational problems when you look at the life of Jacob. As we will encounter in the next chapter, similar favoritism of his own son Joseph resulted in the terrible heartache of losing him for many years to the hatred of Joseph's brothers. Jacob despaired for the emptiness of his life over that loss. It also resulted after the fact in the intractable guilt of initially jealous and vindictive brothers who, at the time, didn't hesitate to sell Joseph to the first trading caravan that came along.

Today we find the same cross-generational phenomena with physical or psychological abuse of one sort or another, alcoholism and drug addictions, and a host of other problems that plague families and, as a result, their progeny. Family histories are important factors precisely because the family, besides providing the genetic pool for certain problems, is an effective incubator of bad habits. Wittingly or unwittingly, parents are teaching their children how to cope with life's problems, if by no other means than by modeling their own coping strategies. So the effects of favoritism can live on in the lives of their children and in the lives of their children's children.

Sadly, sin has a way of covering up its sources, even to those who are engaging in it, or if not covering it up, at least providing a rationale for its presence.

The issues with Isaac and Rebekah stand as proof of that.

***

Points to Ponder

Besides repeating the same mistake his father made with his mother, which undoubtedly caused deep pain and uncertainty for his wife, Isaac dug a new hole for himself when he began giving most of his attention to Esau. It likely angered Rebekah that her son, Jacob, to whom she felt closest, wasn't getting the credit she thought he deserved for being gifted in his own right. Of course, neither of them were doing their boys any favors with their plots and counter-plots to boost the stock of one over the other. In the long run, it only added another layer of disaffection to the dwindling prospects for happiness in their marriage.

This same prejudice in parenting which damaged Isaac and Rebekah's family likewise occurs today, and it is just as destructive now as it was then. The fact is that some children have characteristics that are naturally more attractive to their parents than other children. For instance, some have easygoing personalities and others don't. Some, by their nature, are more obedient and responsive to discipline, while others are more rigid and rebellious. What's more, some are relatively calm and peaceful, while others are noisy and rambunctious, often getting into trouble for their behavior. On top of these differences, children also vary in terms of physical abilities, where some are naturally more athletic, excelling in sports, and others are uncoordinated and have two left feet.

There are myriad reasons why parents can even unwittingly gravitate more toward one child than another. That's why it's important to be aware of such prejudice when it's in play, not only for the sake of your children, but also for the sake of your marriage. In order for marriages and families to strengthen over the course of time, spouses need to be on the same page regarding parenting strategies. Too often one parent is overly permissive while the other is a strict disciplinarian, each trying to compensate for what they see as the weaknesses of the other. This, in turn, creates a resident bitterness that eats away at the heart of the relationship.

As we have seen, the trap of favoring one child over another, as with Isaac and Rebekah, sets up major conflicts between the parents. This is particularly common in blended families where a parent sometimes favors their own biological child over the spouse's child from a previous marriage. Bitter fights often break out, creating a chasm between the spouses, where each sees the other giving preferential treatment to their own biological child. Not a few relationships have imploded over issues like these.

Marriage partners need to feel they are pulling the oars in the same direction. Otherwise, they become frustrated and disheartened, then resentful when nothing seems to change. The kids, too, master the art of playing one parent against the other in order to get their way. So you end up with perpetually resentful parents and highly manipulative children, a losing combination if ever there was one.

What you learn in your home of origin stays with you for a very long time, often getting in the way of finding true happiness. That's especially true when you develop emotional associations to certain circumstances which leave you vulnerable to reacting in dysfunctional ways to similar situations as adults. As a result, you become prone to make the same mistakes your parents did. Or else you make new ones in your determined efforts to separate your response from theirs. Either way, your marriage is likely to be a casualty, which is why it's so important that you have the courage and humility to honestly face your fears. The unexamined life is simply not an option if you want a satisfying marriage.

The example of the relationship between Isaac and Rebekah was given to us, not only to reinforce the lesson about Abraham's fears, but also to show just how destructive prejudicial attitudes can be in both marriage and family. It's not merely an interesting sidelight to the story of redemptive history. Rather, it's a primary lesson on what mistakes to avoid if you want to experience the fullness of a life well-lived.

Chapter 4

Jacob and Leah: When Love is Missing
Genesis 29:14-30:24; 37:1-36; 42-45

The greatest tragedy of Jacob's life was to repeat the parenting mistake of his own mother and father. Of all people, you might think that Jacob would know how destructive favoritism is in a child's life. After all, it took a long time before he and his brother were able to repair their relationship, and then only because each had finally assumed a posture of forgiveness. By then, they each deeply regretted that so much time had passed during which they had no relationship at all.

When God changed Jacob's name, which meant "deceiver", to Israel, which meant, "may God prevail", it was a directive to Jacob to leave behind his tendencies to deceive others and instead to allow God to reshape his person. He was to be the leader of what would become a great nation, so how he led was intended to reflect the transparent righteousness of his Lord.

While in many ways he succeeded in doing just that, his Achilles heel manifested itself in his parenting. Almost immediately after his son Joseph was born, he began favoring him over the others. Why? Because Joseph was the first child born to his beloved wife Rachel.

By bestowing gifts and praise on his new son, Jacob incurred the hardening resentment of his other sons against Joseph, attitudes to which he seemed completely oblivious. As predictable as the sunrise every morning, Jacob's sons came to hate Joseph, much like Esau had earlier come to hate

Jacob, and for the same reason. Is it any surprise that the identical parenting blunder would yield an identical result? All children really want is to be loved equally by their parents. Like adults, children want to feel important, too.

Later, with Joseph presumed dead, Jacob clung tenaciously to Benjamin, his only remaining son by Rachel, during whose birth Rachel had tragically died. Even in the midst of a severe famine in the land, he wouldn't let Benjamin travel with his brothers to Egypt to purchase grain for survival. He didn't want to take the chance that something might happen to him as well.

The fact that his brothers didn't contest his decision and that Judah, in particular, became quite protective of his younger brother, suggests that they had finally figured out why Joseph and Benjamin had been so important to their father. It had nothing to do with them; it was about his deep and abiding love for Rachel.

No doubt this fostered greater empathy toward their father, whom they probably saw as painfully lonely without Rachel at his side. Judah even commented later to Joseph that he feared his father couldn't survive another major loss, and he had long ago surrendered his optimism for living.

Initially it was their intense hatred that prompted Joseph's brothers to sell him into slavery and to falsely claim to their father that he had been killed by a wild animal. However, it became evident to everyone around Jacob that the agony of that loss remained with him for many, many years. It was not until near the end of his life that he learned Joseph was still alive and residing in Egypt as an official there. It was only then that he rediscovered a measure of joy (Gen.45:27-28).

It's tempting to think that during his time in the emotional desert Jacob pondered the similarity of his treatment of Joseph to his own mother's treatment of him and how his brother resented him for it, but, alas, that didn't seem to be the case. He appeared to have been clueless as to how much his other sons hated Joseph for the greater attention he had lavished upon him. What's more, we have no evidence that he ever really learned that lesson.

We'll never know whether Joseph's brothers, laden with guilt as they had been, later confessed their misdeed to their father or whether they decided to file that piece of information in the "No need to hurt him further" drawer. It's highly unlikely that Joseph would have said anything since he was the epitome of mercy and forgiveness. When he revealed his identity to his shocked brothers, who had come to Egypt seeking relief from a terrible famine in Canaan, not realizing their brother was even alive, he told them to tell his father only the good things that had happened (Gen. 42-45).

But the single caution he gave them was significant. He told them that they were not to quarrel with each other on the way back to their father Jacob. Remember, the only thing Joseph had heard his brothers quarrel about concerned who bore the greatest guilt over what they had done to him. His caution to them appeared to mean that all was forgiven, therefore, there was no need to discuss it among themselves any further. Above all, that included discussing it with their father. Joseph was interested only in healing relationships.

It is recorded that when they returned home and after they had revealed to their father that Joseph was still alive, they went on to tell him *"everything Joseph had said to them"* (Gen. 45:24-27). Taking the cue from Joseph there is no indication they talked about the events that happened over twenty years earlier. It wouldn't have substantially benefitted the family. In fact it may have harmed it if they had talked about those things. They all knew their father was in a fragile condition, both emotionally and physically.

In all, Jacob had twelve sons and a daughter, but only two by Rachel. Six of his sons and his only daughter were born to Leah, and four sons, two each, were born to his wives' two maidservants, Bilbah and Zilpah. If anyone would have understood the pain of feeling unloved that Joseph's brothers felt, it would have been Leah. She was keenly aware that Jacob's real love was for Rachel, not her (Gen. 29:26). After all, she was taken to be Jacob's wife only because her father Laban had forced his hand. She knew all too well that Jacob's relationship with Rachel was deeply affectionate and that Rachel enjoyed an intimacy with him that she would never have, even though she bore him more children.

Jacob's relationship with Leah, though respectful and cordial, could never be emotionally fulfilling for her because for him it was essentially platonic. In her early years, she had even entered a contest with Rachel for bearing children, which she had dearly hoped would translate into the love she so desperately wanted from Jacob. But she soon realized that she couldn't really compete with Rachel for his love. She could bear him ten children, even ones who attained great honor, and it wouldn't matter. His love would still belong exclusively to Rachel.

Jacob's favoritism of Joseph, and his attachment to Benjamin, his last child with Rachel, was merely a reminder to her that neither she nor her children would ever occupy the same place in Jacob's heart as her sister and her children. Yes, Jacob was congenial, even considerate, with her; but he was never passionate with her. For the most part, Leah had resigned herself to a loveless but utilitarian marriage that left her bereft of the intimacy she craved.

You can't really blame Jacob for that. From day one, he had professed his love for Rachel and no other. It was her father's cruel and unethical last minute swap that landed her in a marriage that was empty and without affection. She spent her adult life wanting something she knew she could never have. In His compassion, God honored her not merely with many children, but specifically with the birth of Judah, who, in time, became the leader of the family and was the son from whom would come the ancestral line of the Messiah.

During Leah's lifetime, she had to do without a husband's love. Even though she was not abused or ignored, the loss of any chance for marital happiness was hard to endure. Her only consolation was her faith in God. It may be difficult to understand why a father would do that to his daughter, but, in that day, a female dependent was often seen more as a financial liability, especially to men like Laban, who was largely a captive of his darker side. More generally, it was simply an ugly truth of ancient culture.

Still, she made the best of a bad situation and remained a dutiful wife to her husband. It was her steadfast character, despite her unrequited longings, that made her stand out as a faithful follower of the Lord.

We will take a closer look at the other side — the brighter side—of the multi-faceted story of Jacob in a later chapter where the husband's tenderness and affection take center stage. For now, suffice it to say that Rachel's love life came at the expense of Leah's happiness, even though Rachel played no part in the deceit of her father.

***

Points to Ponder

The overriding lesson the story of Jacob and Leah teaches us is that marriage should never be considered if you have any doubts about your love for your partner. That may seem an obvious point, but you might be surprised how many secretly wonder in the back of their minds whether they're really in love with the person they're about to marry and decide to marry anyway.

Perhaps they're too afraid of hurting their fiancé's feelings, disappointing parents or friends, or going against the tide of other people's expectations to honestly reveal their doubts. Maybe they're hesitant because they have feelings for someone else, possibly a former boyfriend or girlfriend with whom they've never achieved closure, or they find themselves more attracted to others than they think they should be.

Whatever the reason for their doubts, they nevertheless believe they are too far into the present relationship to back out now. So, they plunge ahead, doubts and all, without seeking any counsel from a professional or even consulting a confidant.

But if they marry without the full commitment of their love, it may appear, usually in small things at first, once the "honeymoon phase" is over, then eventually in their general attitudes towards the idiosyncrasies of their partner. The things they like about their spouses begin to fade in significance as the things they don't like take on greater weight. They start looking for reasons to complain about them and compare them to others they find more attractive, which can include the wives of other men or husbands of other women.

When a couple like this comes in for counseling, it soon becomes evident that the aggrieved spouse is emotionally distant and behaviorally disengaged, while the other is desperate, completely insecure, yet clueless about what's going on in their marriage. The latter is looking for answers — anything that would explain why their partner is backing away — while the former is looking for reasons to justify leaving the relationship. It's a cruel circumstance that could have been avoided if they had been fully transparent at the beginning before they got married.

Leah's marriage to Jacob underlined the importance of having the unequivocal love of the person you're marrying, because without that, nothing but a life of emptiness lies ahead. It's one of the reasons for having a substantial courtship rather than a whirlwind romance. It's imperative that true love be sifted out and separated from short term infatuation, from intoxicating but misplaced idealism, and from the long-term habituated comfort of familiarity.

The marital union is not about settling for the best available option. It's too sacred for that. If all you seek in love is peace and pleasure, then you are shortchanging love's offering. You see, marriage is a commitment borne on the wings of a love that embraces the whole person, warts and all. It includes the parts you don't like as well as the parts you like. It means holding nothing back in your full-throated acceptance of your loved one. Though we need not be concerned with God's character which is flawless, Jesus perfectly captured the spirit of this kind of devotion when He urged us to love Our Lord "with all our hearts, all our souls, and all our strength" (Mark 12:30). That's the wholeness of genuine love at its most comprehensive level.

When you marry someone you have doubts about but tell yourself you'll change his or her troubling behaviors after you're married, you're unwittingly preparing yourself for disillusionment. That doesn't mean you won't have *self*-doubts at times. Only when we fling ourselves — self-doubts and all — into the game of life can we take the measure of our own trustworthiness.

However, if your doubts are about the other person, then you must shine the light of truth into the dark corners of your unsettled soul to examine what fears or trepidations lurk there. Without unfurling the red flags of caution, we walk in uncertain directions unguided by the compass of wisdom. Too many times in courtship young couples ignore these flags and consequently pay a dear price.

It sometimes humorously said that "women marry expecting their husbands will change but they don't; and men marry expecting their wives to stay the same, but they don't!" Whatever is the case, marriage naturally brings with it a measure of surprise, and that is as it should be. The surprise element is what keeps the relationship fresh, even if it sometimes challenges your coping skills. Love is not only for your growth; it's also for your pruning.

When you utter the words, "for better or worse", it is an admission that you're likely to encounter bad times as well as good times, but your love should be greater than both. Marriage is neither an experiment nor a "wait and see" arrangement. Jesus constantly talked about the permanence of marriage because He knew that it was, above all, a spiritual union, which God Himself ordained. That's why the wedding vows often end with the words, "what God has joined together, let not man put asunder" (Matt. 19:6). Never forget that divorce is trifling with God's work.

Both Rachel's and Leah's marriages mirrored this principle, but the differences of their experiences in them reflect the pivotal role that a thoroughly genuine love, constantly cultivated, must play to make any marriage fulfilling. For joy and contentment to last beyond the moment, it must be shared. Leah had no one to share them with. Only Rachel did.

Leah had no choice in selecting her mate. Common in the marriages of the ancient Near East, her father Laban made the choice for her, unfortunately for Leah, one that was based solely on what was materially advantageous for him. Love and courtship had nothing to do with it. As a result, Leah lost out on her chance for happiness.

Women today, at least those in the West, are free to choose whomever they wish to marry. Yet either because their perception is distorted by their own dysfunction, or because they simply ignored the red flags during their courtship, many of them end up marrying poorly anyway.

When such women are later asked in counseling if they saw the red flags in their partner's behavior while they were dating, the large majority indicate that they did. When asked why they ignored those red flags, they often respond by telling the counselor that they thought the behaviors in question weren't that important at the time, or that things would be different after they got married. Not surprisingly, that didn't happen. It's often the case that those same behaviors become increasingly front and center in their marriage. The normal demands of children who come along in the family usually only make these flaws and inadequacies more evident.

Since attitudes of good will are more likely to exist during courtship than later down the road when the marriage is in trouble, it's better to tackle these issues prior to marriage when you still have options before things escalate out of control.

These sorts of considerations were a moot point for most of the women in the Old Testament, who lived in times where they had few rights and little say in decisions that profoundly affected their lives. Sadly, it was not uncommon for some of them to become trapped in dictatorial relationships with evil and disreputable men who had the wherewithal to strike lucrative deals with their fathers. Or, as was true in Leah's case, being unwittingly shanghaied by a scheming father who cheated a suitor for one daughter into taking the other as well, which was more than he bargained for. Whatever the circumstance, many of these wives were then forced to live with husbands who didn't love them and treated them with relative indifference, if not outright contempt.

Being stuck in a bad marriage can still be true today, but women now have other options. For the most part, in the Western world, the patriarchal system with its arranged marriages is gone, having been replaced by greater equality and fairer treatment in relationships, thanks largely to the Christian notion of liberty.

Unfortunately, that freedom doesn't stop people from making bad choices in courtship, nor does it prevent the disillusionment for which their denial paves the way. Still, God in His mercy has provided us with the story of Jacob and Leah to remind us of the care we should take in choosing mates who genuinely love us. The consequences of failing to heed this caution can be devastating.

All the more reason for spouses not to abuse the privileges that liberty provides.

Part Three - Heartless Marriages

Chapter 5

Nabal and Abigail: When Basic Respect is Missing
1Samuel 25:1-44

A quite different example of a loveless relationship is found in the marriage of Nabal and Abigail. Like other women of the day, Abigail was likely given in marriage to Nabal by her father who was more interested in her material welfare and his own family's financial security than he was in her happiness. Such marriages were more like business transactions between families than anything resembling romantic courtships. Like Leah, Abigail undoubtedly had little say in the marital arrangement.

She was described as beautiful, discerning, and socially adept, no doubt satisfying both Nabal's lust and his powerful desire to showcase his social standing. Abigail was the perfect trophy wife. Her dutifulness as a wife served as a counterweight to his narcissistic, surly character; he strutted about in the material trappings of his immense wealth, lording it over everyone else. The world was there to serve him, not the other way around. He ate to excess, he drank to excess, and he partied to excess. He was a man of intemperate tastes and of foul disposition. The fact that his name meant "fool" fit perfectly with his personality and with his harsh, antagonistic behavior toward others. Nabal was someone you wouldn't want to spend five minutes with.

Since Abigail was stuck with him, she tried her best to make things as manageable as possible under the circumstances. It wasn't easy constantly smoothing over the agitated feelings the boorish Nabal left in his wake. By the time David ran into her, she was exhausted trying to run interference for a husband who couldn't care less about who he insulted. It didn't matter if they were common peasants or local officials; he was uniformly rude to them all.

Because he had a lot of money, he carried a lot of power, which he routinely exercised in an abusive way. No one who knew him liked him, not even his employees, but it didn't concern him in the least, since he was contemptuous of almost everyone anyway. The only reason people came to his parties or listened to what he had to say was because money talks and Nabal knew it.

Though he benefitted from their services, he was predictably ungrateful to anyone who volunteered their help, including those who protected his property, which brings us to his interactions with David. At the time, David was running a fugitive operation, keeping himself at arm's length from King Saul, who was chasing him around Judea determined to kill him. David, meanwhile, protected the locals from being harmed by their traditional enemies, including an assortment of raiders and thieves.

After defeating these miscreants in various skirmishes, David handed over a large portion of the spoils he gained to those whom he was protecting. All he asked for in return was for provisions to feed his men. It was common practice for wealthy landowners to honor this minimal request by those who guarded their property. To be sure, the general populace loved him for it, especially since many of the farmers and sheepherders in the area were struggling to eke out a living in the midst of a war against the Philistines. But not Nabal. Instead, he huffed, *"Who is this son of Jesse? Many servants are breaking away from their masters these days. Why should I take my bread and water and the meat I've slaughtered for my shearers, and give it to men coming from who knows where"* (1 Sam. 25: 10-11).

What made this response especially contemptible was the report of one of Nabal's servants, who informed Abigail that Nabal had hurled insults at David's men and refused to give them provisions, even though they had formed "a wall "of protection around them all the time they were out in the field shepherding their sheep. The servant concluded with this desperate plea: *"Now think it over and see what you can do, because disaster is hanging over our master and his whole household. He is such a wicked man that no one can talk to him"* (vs. 17).

When the men who had gone to Nabal asking for provisions returned to David with the message that he had refused their request, David immediately ordered his men to put on their swords. Taking 400 men with him, he set out for Nabal's territory, fully intending to take Nabal down. Meanwhile, Abigail, livid over her husband's behavior, lost no time gathering together a bountiful supply of foodstuffs and rushing out to meet David to plead for his forbearance.

Taking the blame on herself for what had happened, she begged David not to pay any heed to "that wicked man" Nabal, but to take her gift of appreciation as compensation for his heroic work on her household's behalf. She was banking on David's reputation for kindness and sense of fair play to win the day, which is why she made a point to remind David that the Lord had, up until then, kept him from "avenging himself with his own hands," so surely he would keep him from any wrongdoing in the future.

It was both a brilliant move and a godly stance. By invoking God's hand over David, she had reminded him that he had been blessed for following the Lord's commands and that it would be a shame if he resorted to unnecessary violence now. Impressed by Abigail's wisdom and convicted by the oath he had given to serve the Lord, David responded by telling her that only by her last minute intervention did God keep him from harming her servants. Accepting her gift, he then turned around and returned to his camp. Abigail had saved David from taking an action of retribution that he would have deeply regretted later.

Shortly after this, she went to her husband intending to tell him everything. Instead, she decided to wait until morning because he was, yet again, very drunk at one of his self-serving banquets. The next day, after he had sobered up, she explained to him what she had done. Becoming enraged upon hearing what had happened behind his back, he suddenly clutched his chest, struck by a massive heart attack. He died some ten days later. Apprised of this welcome news, David sent word that he wanted to take her as his wife. Abigail spent the rest of her days among the royal entourage, finally living with someone who appreciated her for who she was.

Nabal's and Abigail's marriage is the story of an astute woman who, despite the harsh, demeaning behavior of the tyrant she called her husband, used her wise and discerning spirit to rescue her household from certain disaster. She was not afraid to be assertive when the situation called for it, yet she always respected the position of her husband, even if she didn't respect him as a person.

Apparently, she also had won the respect and trust of both the household and field servants, since they felt free to come to her to discuss problems her husband was causing. Indeed, they must have sensed that Abigail was discerning enough to understand their dilemma and not reflexively defend her husband no matter how abusive, demeaning, and insulting his behavior was.

Think about that for a moment. In a society where the influence and judgment of women was considered inferior to that of men, these servants chose to come to *her* for advice. She quickly sized up the situation that Nabal had put them in and, knowing there was no chance that her arrogant husband would ever apologize to David, she swung into the damage control mode in which she had likely found herself on numerous occasions before.

She seemed to know that David was a godly man, whether or not she knew he would be king one day. Her judgment, as it turned out, was impeccable. Though David was a fugitive, running from the king of Israel, she had to make a decision based on whatever limited information she had of him that he was an honorable man and would do the right thing if given the right advice. Trusting her intuitive wisdom, she took the risk and made her move. It proved conclusively to be the right one.

***

Points to Ponder

Abigail demonstrated a number of admirable qualities that apply well to spouses today, despite the fact that she lived in a deeply troublesome marriage which was not of her own choosing, but divorce in those days would have greatly imperiled her survival and that of her children. Nevertheless, she didn't stay in her marriage because of his wealth; she stayed because that was what was expected of a woman in that culture. Any alternative would have been met with suspicion about her character, which would have greatly limited her chances of mercy from the surrounding community and, perhaps, even her clan.

She showed humility both in her choice of words to David and her refusal to slander her husband in front of his servants. She had a quiet but determined deference about her that was disarming to others. She engaged in neither the arrogance of her husband nor the defiance of someone out to put others in their place.

There appeared to be no need to become defensive around her. When one of the servants approached her about a problem with her husband, she didn't excoriate him for lodging his complaint. Neither did she proceed to express to him how she really felt about her husband, though the servants had probably already surmised as much. Instead, she thanked him for letting her know and immediately turned her attention to determining the next steps to take.

That's what true assertiveness looks like. When your actions are based on the acknowledgement that problems need to be proactively solved, not reactively exploited by the self-righteous attitude of a victim, you save your marriage a lot of wear and tear. It's not about complaining about how horrible things are, but rather about determining what can be done to make things better. In most marital conflicts, that requires the humility to admit that because you are part of the problem you must also be a part of the solution.

Instead of trying to avoid confronting the problem, do you invite your spouse to openly discuss it? Do you do this with the promise to explore the issues calmly and honestly, with an eye toward how each can help to make it work? That's not as easy as it sounds when emotions are running high, but it's necessary if you intend to find out what each of you wants or needs and to make certain these things are properly addressed before you're done.

It's interesting to note that Abigail went directly to her husband and told him what she had done. She wanted everything to be out in the open. She had nothing to hide, no secret alliances, no clandestine operations, just honest self-disclosure. Relationships that hold all sorts of secrets become demonstrably toxic over time — and in her case would've become even worse than it already was. They can become explosive, too, maybe even deal breakers, if one of those secrets is inadvertently exposed.

It's important to remember that transparency is the hallmark of a healthy marriage. When you commit yourself to your partner, you are saying you want that person to know you better than anyone else on earth. It's what leads to trust, which leads to greater intimacy. Though it's what people *say* they really want, they are often reluctant to take the risk because they've been taught to believe that such risk — any risk — is too great.

Note also that Abigail patiently waited to tell Nabal what she had done until he was clear enough of mind to understand exactly what she was saying. Knowing his sour demeanor when he was sober, it might have been tempting to tell him when he was drunk and in high spirits, that is, when he was less likely to respond negatively (or, at least, coherently) to her revelation. Once again, it speaks to her honesty that she wanted him to fully understand her actions, knowing it would likely incur blowback of some sort. She opted for honesty with repercussions over dishonesty which carried with it the burden of doing everything behind his back. Besides, she knew he was likely to find out eventually anyway.

Finally, others have pointed out that Abigail was especially adept at choosing her words carefully, speaking with the clarity of her reasoning rather than with the volatility of her emotions. This is important because the person listening to you can hear your words at a faster rate than you can say them. That means there is a time lag during which the listener's thoughts can sweep past the words you speak, affecting the meaning they derive from what you're saying. If you let your emotions do all the talking, it will arouse the listener's defenses to the point that his interfering thoughts will be more emotion-laden and more distracting from the words you're actually speaking.

If in your anger you come out swinging, or if in your panic you come out demanding, you'll almost certainly shut down the other person's ability to hear what you have to say. If you want them to understand you, first you must come across as non-threatening, even deferential, as did Abigail with David, whom she knew was already arriving with a chip on his shoulder. Calm is only restored when you appeal to their better nature.

Some years ago, a small book on business communications, entitled, *The First Five Minutes*[3] was published which maintained that the first few minutes of every human transaction determines the quality of the communication thereafter. If you start out on a pleasing note, whether it's how you present yourself or what mood you display or what courtesies you extend to the other person, the remainder of the interaction is much more likely to end positively. But if you start out on a sour note which emotionally distances your colleague the interaction is far more likely to end up negatively. Certainly, the latter is magnified when you're depressed or angry or complaining to others around you. This is called the "halo effect" of first impressions in the process of communication and it applies to any occasion of human interaction, including that of married couples. Its impact can last the rest of the day or evening or, in the case of business relations, even longer. So, how you begin is crucial to how you end.

It's useful, for example, to ask yourself how you greet your spouse after a long day apart. Is it a recitation of everything that went wrong during your day, maybe including complaints about your boss or a co-worker or griping

---

[3] Mitchell, Mary, with John Corr, "The First Five Minutes: How to Make a Great First Impression in Any Business Situation", Trade Press, May, 1998.

about the rush hour traffic coming home? Or is it a smiling declaration about how good it is to be back together again with your spouse, even if it was a rough day? The beginning of your evening makes all the difference to how your mate responds to you later on.

Judging how she handled the delicate interaction with David, Abigail knew well how to effectively defuse a potentially incendiary situation. So much so that David was impressed enough to ask for her hand in marriage after Nabal had died.

Of course, having been married to Nabal for many years, she undoubtedly had had plenty of experience learning how to gracefully exit interpersonal conflict. It's probably the only positive thing she could take away from a first marriage like hers. Still, her ability to make the best of every situation, gave her an advantage others, like Nabal, didn't have.

We learn from this that regardless of position in life the exercise of judicious wisdom, not reactive outrage, will be the difference that likely carries the day.

Chapter 6

David and Michal: Hitting below the Belt
1Samuel 18:20-29; 19:11-18; 2Samuel 6:16-23

The marriage of David and Michal is, perhaps, one of the saddest accounts of a marriage in the Bible, despite beginning on a high note. Michal was passionately in love with David (1 Sam.18:20). Interestingly, it's the only time in the Old Testament where there is mention of a woman loving a man. Michal envisioned a storybook marriage where the beautiful young princess is swept away by her dashing military officer hero.

Although it was true that Michal's father King Saul felt threatened by David's military success and evident popularity among the people of Israel, his fear led him to offer the hand of his daughter in marriage. He did this on the promise that David would "bravely fight the battles of the Lord", but underneath, Saul hoped David would become a casualty of the war, thereby eliminating his competition for military glory.

Humbled by the offer, David had replied that he was a poor man, suggesting he didn't have the resources to afford the bridal price that usually comes with such a marriage. But Saul countered David's expression of unworthiness by telling him that he wanted no other price than a hundred Philistine foreskins, appealing to his honor as a commander in Saul's army.

The only hiccup for Michal was that Saul had in mind his older daughter Merab, not her, but when it came time for Merab to be given to David, she had already been given in marriage to another man, Ariel of Meholah. Fortunately for Michal, Saul changed his mind as to whom he would give to

David. It's entirely possible he was persuaded by the deep love his younger daughter had for him, which was apparently obvious to everyone around her.

Michal, to her delight, became the prize for the handsome, charismatic young warrior. Fortunately, David was likewise attracted to Michal, or at least he appeared to be, though some have argued not to the same degree. It's recorded that "he was pleased to become the king's son-in-law", not only because of the position it gave him but also for the woman he was about to receive in the exchange. It seemed, from the outset that it would be the perfect marriage.

As mentioned earlier, by offering his daughter, Saul was considerably less gracious toward David than it appeared on the surface. Instead, he was rather cunning, even diabolical, in his thinking. Premised on the principle, "keep your friends close and your enemies closer", he wanted David to join the royal family mainly because David would then feel obligated to fight for the king on the front lines, where he would be more likely killed in action. "I will not raise a hand against him," Saul thought to himself. "Let the Philistines do that!" (1 Sam. 18: 17).

But the lionhearted David proved to be such a brilliant military leader that he consistently routed the Philistines in battle after battle without sustaining so much as a scratch, much to Saul's chagrin. He didn't merely return with a hundred Philistine foreskins; he presented the king with twice that many!

Realizing his plan had backfired, and now unable to refuse David marriage to his daughter, which gave David even greater authority in the public's eye as a member of the royal family, Saul became trapped in his rising tide of paranoia. Adding this turn of events to the fact that he knew the Lord was with David but had left him, he became increasingly desperate to rid himself of his competitor for the nation's affections. When he learned that his son Jonathon, Michal's brother, also loved David, and fiercely defended him at every turn, it was the final straw. Saul simply snapped, no longer constrained by even the faintest appearance of reason.

Once it became publicly known that his father-in-law hated David, a tense cat-and-mouse game commenced between the two, ironically giving Michal the opportunity to play the role of the heroine for her man. Saul had sent men to David's house to surveil it until morning, with orders to kill him at daybreak. When Michal learned of her father's plan, she rushed to David and warned him to run for his life. Presumably using a rope and perhaps a basket, she lowered David to the ground through an upper window outside behind their home. He disappeared into the night, safely escaping his assassins who were in front, lying in wait for him.

Michal did not flee with David, opting to remain at the house to confront Saul's soldiers, giving David more time to make his escape. That's the last she was to see or hear from her beloved husband for months, even years. When the soldiers demanded to see David, whom she said was ill, in bed, and couldn't be disturbed, she finally relented and ushered them to his bedroom. There she had cleverly laid a *terraphim* (a household idol Jews pretended to represent God) on the bed covered over by a blanket with some goat's hair at the head to give the appearance of a man sleeping.

After getting a glimpse of the room, they were quietly led back to the front door and they returned to Saul and reported what they had found. Saul was outraged, sending his men back to David's home, this time to arrest him and bring him back to the palace, on a stretcher if need be.

When the soldiers realized they had been tricked, they grabbed Michal and dragged her back to stand before her father. The livid Saul demanded how she could betray her own father, but Michal lied and told her father that she covered for David only because he had threatened her life if she didn't comply with his demands. This explanation assuaged Saul's anger toward her, but only increased his determination to kill David.

Meanwhile, David made no attempt to contact Michal, if only to let her know that he was okay and hoped to send for her soon. As his silence dragged on for months and then years, she felt completely abandoned, and likely believed he no longer loved her, if he ever did.

During this time, King Saul concluded that David's marriage to Michal was never legal, believing that the Philistine foreskins had no monetary value to qualify for any transactional validity. Whether for that reason or for some other, Saul was looking for grounds — any ground — to invalidate David's relationship to his daughter and, therefore depriving him of using his affiliation with the royal family as a source of authority or as a pretense to the crown in the future.

Satisfied that he had found a rationale others could buy into, King Saul settled on a man named Paltiel (also referred to as Palti), son of Laish, to whom he offered the hand of Michal in marriage. Paltiel lived in the nearby town of Gallim and was believed to have been a chieftain or an otherwise important local figure of some sort. Apparently, he had long admired Michal from afar and, had it not been for the fact that she was part of the royal family, probably would have courted her before she married David. For Saul's part, however, it was an act of spite, in which he was announcing to the nation his final break with David.

Over time, Michal would most likely have heard that David had taken other wives in her absence (Abigail and Ahinoam), confirming to her that the relationship they'd had with each other was over. The bitterness of that reality must have weighed heavily upon her. On the other hand, it was plain to see that Paltiel really loved her and had committed himself to her happiness. As the years rolled by, that bitterness would doubtless have abated, as did any remaining feelings she had for David.

Both biblical scholars and rabbinical sources have suggested, however, that Paltiel never had sexual relations with Michal, since it was unclear whether she was still married to David. He wanted to avoid committing adultery, for which he might be roundly condemned, at least by those in his community who were unfamiliar with what had happened behind the scenes.

But the story of Michal's marriage to David was not finished.

After King Saul's death, with his lone surviving son 40-year-old Ishbosheth now on the throne, war broke out with Judah because the Judahites refused to recognize him as king. Instead, they seceded from the house of Saul and set up their own kingdom in Hebron with David at its head. As it turned out, Ishbosheth proved to be an ineffectual weakling whose only accomplishment was to make an enemy out of his own commander-in-chief, Abner. As a consequence, Abner made overtures to David, promising to bring with him the rest of the nation of Israel if they could reach an agreement.

David consented to the alliance, provided that he would take Saul's daughter Michal away from Paltiel and restore her to him as his wife. When Ishbosheth, anxious to avoid further war, received word directly from David's messengers that David was demanding the return of Michal, he quickly moved to take her away from Paltiel: "*So, Ishbosheth gave orders and had her taken from her husband, Paltiel son of Laish. Her husband, however, went with her, weeping behind her all the way to Bahurim. Then Abner said to him, 'Go back home!' So, he went back*" (2 Sam. 3: 15-16).

It was a heart-wrenching picture of a broken-hearted man who seemed to be lovingly devoted to Michal yet was being forced to give her up against his will. There is no mention here what Michal was feeling, but given Paltiel's unquestioned love for her and David's long absence from her, it's not hard to imagine she had a lot of misgivings about being taken away from Paltiel. It's highly doubtful she felt good about going back to David, especially without any evidence he wanted her back because he still loved her.

For a long time now, she had experienced Paltiel's love and devotion, a comfortable living, and a stable home. Why would she want to give all that up to join the growing list of David's wives? After all, it was obvious that as her love for David had faded with time so did her hope that he really wanted her.

The question was whether she could ever re-ignite her first love for him. Of course, she couldn't know whether David still felt affection for her or whether he simply wanted her for the political value of being connected to the house of Saul, which might smooth the transition to a unified monarchy and strengthen his claim to the throne.

When word came that Ishbosheth had been assassinated and that the path was clear to unite the northern and southern tribes, this question was about to be put to the test. One thing was clear: The reunion of David and Michal was going to begin on uncertain grounds. It wasn't long, however, before she learned whether her marriage to David had any sustainability.

With the people once again united under a single crown head, David decided to relocate his capital to Jerusalem, which straddled the middle ground between the tribes of Judah and Benjamin and the rest of the tribes in the north. He ordered the Ark of the Covenant be brought there as well. He wanted his capital to be a religious center as well as a political one. It was, as it turned out, a stroke of genius to bring the principal symbol of God's presence to the city as a move to unify the people around their common faith. It was important to David that God was front and center in his kingdom.

As they brought the Ark into Jerusalem with a grand procession and with great fanfare, complete with shouts of the priests and the sound of trumpets, the king began wildly dancing in celebration. With his robes cast aside and his ephod flapping in the air, he danced with all his might. Meanwhile, Michal was watching the entire affair from the window of their living quarters. It's recorded that "when she saw King David leaping and dancing before the Lord, she despised him in her heart" (2 Sam. 6: 16). It deeply embarrassed her that he had dropped all pretense of royal decorum, and became the picture of uninhibited emotion. To her, it bordered on indecency.

Michal was a very private person who had a strong conservative bent and preferred to express her passion in seclusion. Having grown up in a royal family, she had a certain concept of how a king should comport himself, even though her father was hardly a useful model of rationality. In fact, his volatility may have contributed to her view of the importance of propriety in royal conduct. In any event, Michal was not the least bit happy at what she saw David doing as he led the procession celebrating the arrival of the Ark of the Covenant.

When David returned home that evening to bless his household, Michal made known her disgust at his behavior: *"How the king of Israel distinguished himself today, disrobing in the sight of the slave girls of his servants as any vulgar fellow would!"* (2 Sam. 6: 20).

Michal had maligned his motive of holy zeal to be little more than theatrical vulgarity, an accusation that clearly cut to the quick. David turned ashen with rage. He was not about to let her sarcastic shaming pass. At first, David rightly defended his actions, arguing he had done nothing wrong, but then he hit below the belt, too. He shot back an incredibly cruel response that must have emotionally leveled Michal, with every biting word hitting her like hammer blows to the head:

> *"It was before the Lord, who chose me rather than your father or anyone from his house when he appointed me ruler over the Lord's people Israel—I will celebrate before the Lord. I will become even more undignified than this, and I will be humiliated in my own eyes. But by these slave girls you spoke of, I will be held in honor"* (2 Sam. 6:21-22).

We are not told how Michal responded to his seething rebuttal. Perhaps that was because she likely fell completely silent as she nursed her own emotional wounds. Though no formal divorce was ever filed, probably because of the potential political ramifications involved, this devastating interaction effectively brought the marriage of David and Michal to an ignominious end. From that point on, it remained in a state of living death.

The epitaph was given in a single cryptic remark: "And Michal, daughter of Saul, had no children to the day of her death" (vs. 23). In other words, David never went to her again. Isolated and alone, she spent the rest of her days essentially a prisoner in the solitary confinement of her own apartment in the palace complex. There she could only ruminate over her hopeless life without the affection and genuine care of her loving companion, Paltiel.

For her, it was paradise lost.

***

Points to Ponder

Words matter. The words you choose to communicate your displeasure over something your marriage partner has said or done are crucial to the outcome of the interaction. If you come out swinging before your spouse even knows you're angry, such as Michal did, your chances of getting a fair hearing are minimal. Instead, either a shouting match or stone silence will ensue, with both parties walking away wounded from the wreckage of the interaction.

When Michal made her accusations of inappropriate behavior as soon as David walked through the door, before he could even take off his tunic, she had defeated her own purpose. It was only made worse by using derisive words that were not only unfair, but also were dripping with sarcasm. Letting her emotions do all the talking instead of choosing her words more carefully cost her any legitimacy she thought her argument had.

All she succeeded in doing was to put David on the defensive, making her disgust and resentment the center of his attention, not the underlying subject of her distress. She had deeply hurt him when she, in essence, sucker punched him with an attack on his integrity — an attack which came out of the blue the moment he stepped in the apartment.

Almost reflexively, he returned fire, feeling immediately under assault for celebrating, of all things, the arrival of the Ark of the Covenant. No doubt he felt fully justified in his rebuttal because he believed he was being criticized for doing something that was pleasing to God. If he had stopped there, he would have successfully held the moral high ground.

Unfortunately, in his rage he failed to see that by carrying it further and hitting her below the belt as well, he had merely stooped to her level of retaliation. God would have been just as displeased with his response as He was with hers.

There is a reason that God has said, "Revenge is mine". He knows sinful man doesn't have the kind of self-control to know how to handle it righteously. Only He is capable of that. That's why He repeatedly tells us to leave that sort of thing to Him. Peter was quite explicit about this point in advocating that we follow in Jesus' footsteps: *"When they hurled their insults at him, he did not retaliate; when he suffered, he made no threats. Instead, he trusted himself to him who judges justly"* (1 Peter 2: 23, emphasis added).

If only David had done this he would have kept his foothold on the truth of his celebration before the Lord. But in his self-righteous indignation all he wanted to do was hurt Michal in return.

He wasn't really interested in hearing in more detail about what her problem was or what their differences were. Nor was he in the mood to smooth over her ruffled feathers, or at the very least, see if they could find some common ground. No. Instead, he hit her where he knew it hurt the most, denigrating her father and her family and gloating over the fact that God had chosen him to be king over the house of Saul.

Think about that for a moment. Michal had, not long before, lost her father and three of her brothers, all of whom came to violent ends. For all their faults, they were dear to her; they were her family. She was possibly still grieving their loss. At the very least, their deaths were painfully sad memories for her, and now her husband was savaging them and rubbing her nose in their misguided notions of rule. It's hard to think of a faster way to emotionally beat your wife to a pulp than to do what David did.

As far as we know, neither of them ever apologized to the other for the way they responded to each other. In fact, later when the Gibeonites demanded retaliation for Saul's treatment of them during his reign, David readily had the five sons of Merab and Adriel executed to satisfy them, apparently without even consulting Michal. Remember Merab was Michal's older sister, so these young men were her nephews. Consequently, Michal ended up with still more family losses over which she was forced to grieve.

In all fairness, we don't know if Michal was ever given the chance to apologize or clarify her remarks or, if she had, whether she would have seized the opportunity. To our knowledge, they simply parted ways without ever seeking redress of their grievances. It clearly stands as one of the most unnecessary marital ruptures described in the Bible.

Their marriage was the epitome of poor conflict resolution skills on display. Michal violated the basic principle of framing differences in positive terms so that David could have felt that his views or convictions were worthy of respect, even if she didn't necessarily agree with them. Instead of softly speaking about her discomfort, in her anger she unwisely chose the pejorative words of disapproval and disdain.

When you air your differences in positive, negotiable terms, language that encourages each other to enter the conversation as moral equals, you're far more likely to arrive at constructive conclusions. But the minute it degenerates into accusations, name-calling, contempt and sarcasm or worse, where each assumes their position is superior to the other's, any potential for conflict resolution is instantly lost. The purpose of problem solving is not to hammer your spouse into conformity to your point of view, but to work with each other to find solutions that honor the thoughts and feelings of both.

It would have been better if Michal had said something like, "I know that with your great zeal for the Lord how excited you must have been to see the Ark of the Covenant arrive in the city and that was, no doubt, why you celebrated with such exuberance today. But you know me. I'm a very private person who gets easily embarrassed by public displays of excitement. If you wouldn't mind, could we talk about that?" No accusations. Just statements and an invitation to talk. David, in all likelihood, would have been much more willing to hear her out under those circumstances.

But once under attack, David instead violated the principle of temperance in his response to Michal. If his intent was solely to emotionally destroy her, he undoubtedly accomplished his purpose. But if that was the case, it speaks to his lack of self-control. His retort was characteristic of someone who was rarely questioned or criticized, like, say, a king… and by a woman, who in ancient Jewish society didn't enjoy much respect in the first place; that only made it worse.

That said, David had little excuse to treat Michal the way he did. To be sure, he had every right to properly defend himself from her scurrilous accusations, especially where it concerned his celebration of God's goodness, but he could have responded in disagreement without hitting back where she was most vulnerable to being hurt. Hitting below the belt is never the mark of integrity, which was particularly ironic since it was his integrity that was unfairly under attack.

It would have been better had David said something like, "Yeah, I know you're kind of shy about that sort of thing. If it was a bit over the top, I'm sorry if it embarrassed you. But I felt that today needed special recognition and celebration and that it was important to show the people the importance of the presence of God among our people. If you felt I got carried away with that, we can talk about it to see if there is any way you might feel more comfortable." No counter-attacks, just identifying Michal's discomfort and offering an invitation to talk about it.

Notice in both cases there are no personal rebukes, only honest self-disclosure. Instead of disapproval, Michal would be expressing her discomfort. Rather than disparaging Michal's family, David would be pinpointing the issue at hand. It's much easier to see how constructive conversation could have followed such an exchange.

Some might think that Michal simply got what she deserved. If you're going to play smash mouth politics, then you better expect it's going to get ugly. But, as Peter pointed out, that's not what Jesus taught, nor was it the way He responded to similar attacks on His own person. It was the power of His love that turned away malice, not acts of divine retribution.

It's a shame neither David nor Michal had the wisdom to know that "a soft answer turns away wrath, but a harsh word stirs up anger" (Prov. 15: 1), or that "whoever is slow to anger is better than the mighty and he who rules his spirit than he who takes a city" (Prov. 16: 32). But, alas, David didn't always possess the wisdom his son one day would enjoy. Nor did Michal have the advantage of learning better ways to respond from her volatile father. They both would have benefitted had they avoided the pitfall expressed in the proverb which asserts that "a fool takes no pleasure in understanding, but only in expressing his opinion" (Prov. 18: 2).

While the text does not reveal whether David was shouting or not, the tone of his words was filled with rage and contempt. It's likely that he raised his voice in the process. There is an axiom about the volume of one's voice that's wise to heed but is usually ignored in these situations. It argues that there is an inverse proportional relationship between the decibel level of your voice and the credibility of your message: The louder you become, the less believable your message. It's merely one more way to defeat yourself regardless how strong you think your argument is.

Self-righteous indignation is a poor substitute for constructive solutions. No matter how much you think you are in the right, you destroy any potential for good the moment you assume the role of emotional executioner. When the Apostle Paul wrote about the importance of speaking the truth in love, he was encouraging us to avoid the very kinds of tactics that David and Michal used to decimate their relationship. He went on to provide the template for successful interactions in virtually any relationship:

"Do not let any unwholesome talk come out of your mouths, but only what is helpful for building others up according to their needs, that it may benefit those who listen.......Get rid of all bitterness, rage, and anger, brawling and slander, along with every form of malice. Be kind and compassionate to one another, forgiving each other, just as, in Christ, God forgave you" (Eph. 4: 29, 31-32).

We may add to this exhortation the importance of restraint when you're emotionally aroused and in danger of losing control. If you have to, use the so-called "lifesaver technique", which is simple but remarkably effective. It merely requires you, before you can respond in anger, to suck on your favorite-tasting lifesaver until it's gone. In that way you buy the time it takes to cool down enough to speak more softly, without the shrill tones of your rage.

What's more, the sugar in the lifesaver stimulates "hedonic hotspots" in the pleasure centers in the brain which crowd out the limbic system signals (that govern your anger), suppressing or, at least mitigating the emotional response. Because of how your neural networks function, your frontal cortex needs the time to respond, since it takes your rationality much longer to kick in than your emotions, which are automatic and visceral.

The point is you must do all you can to limit the long-lasting damage your immediate reactions can have on your relationships. Otherwise, you're likely facing a lifetime of remorse and regret, or if not these reactions, a lifetime of bitterness. Either way, the result will not be a happy one.

It's a pity we spend so little time listening and so much time talking. Perhaps that's why there are so many passages in Scripture that admonish us to be quick to listen and slow to speak (Prov. 17: 28; 18: 23; James 1: 19). It's our speaking — the words we use — that gets us into trouble, not our listening skills. Think of the sorrows we would keep away from our door if we actually listened more than we spoke!

It would be a good thing if we all practiced that counsel more often. But even casual observation affirms that most social interactions are like presumptive posts on social media. Good listening skills are unfortunately in rare supply. Instead, people constantly make assertions based more on preconceived ideas than on objective evidence.

Is it any wonder then that our society has become so divided?

Chapter 7

Ahab and Jezebel: When Evil Meets Petulance
1Kings 16:29-33; 18:2-4; 19:1-5; 21:1-28; 2Kings 9: 30-37

A hab and Jezebel were well known as one of the most morally corrupt couples to walk across the pages of the Old Testament. Ahab grew up in the palace of his father, Omri. He was used to getting what he wanted when he wanted it. Behind his façade of bravado was a man who was actually weak and cowardly, a man given to whim, yet afraid to take command of a situation unless reassured that others had his back. A crusader for good he was not.

At first he conveniently embraced some of the Abrahamic traditions, albeit only loosely, but he quickly caved to the powerful forces of moral depravity. After all, he was merely following the model of his father Omri, who did much evil in the sight of the Lord. Ahab continued in his father's footsteps despite the fact that Jehovah God had — not once but twice — delivered him from his Syrian enemies. In Ahab's time, there was a serious cultural battle going on for the soul of the nation between the traditional forces of faith in Yahweh and the idolatry of the Ba'als that his wife, Jezebel, introduced. She was the daughter of Ethbaal, the King of the Sidonians.

Without a doubt, she ruthlessly used her power to get whatever she wanted. She was extremely controlling as Ahab's wife, forever dictating to him what he and others should do, and taking her revenge on anyone who opposed her husband and the power of the throne. To that end, she was solely responsible for the deaths of hundreds of God's prophets. Only those who were rescued and hidden in caves by Obadiah, the godly chief of staff of Ahab's palace, survived her bloody hand. It's impossible to overstate her corrupting influence on the nation of Israel and its morally compromised king. Ahab bears no less responsibility for becoming a puppet of her whims in his pursuit of idolatry.

It was during Ahab's reign that Benhadad, King of Syria, envying the riches of Samaria, decided to go to war against Israel (1Kings 20). After gathering an enormous army augmented by the armies of thirty-two neighboring chiefs, he laid siege on Samaria. He even sent a taunting message to Ahab stating that "'...your silver and your gold are mine and your wives and your children are mine also!" (1Kings 20:3).

The frightened Ahab immediately gave in to the demand and sent Benhadad word seeking to appease him. Only when the king of Syria further demanded access to Ahab's palace to take away anything he wanted did Ahab withdraw his offer of appeasement, and then only after consultation with the elders. He was also encouraged to resist by a visit from a prophet of God, who had appeared before him and promised that God had assured his victory (1Kings 20:13-16). What followed was a surprise attack that caught Benhadad and his army off guard, causing them to quickly scatter and flee back to their homes (vs. 19-21).

A year later and after his defeat by Ahab's army in the mountains, Benhadad was convinced he could win in a battle on the plains. He came with another massive army that far outmanned Israel's, but once again the anonymous prophet of God reassured Ahab that victory lay on his side, and once again, he won in impressive fashion (vs. 28).

You might think that having a front row seat in witnessing the display of God's power would have proved to Ahab the prudence of returning to the historic faith of Israel. But no, his wife's influence on him was much too powerful for him to take a different path. Instead, he built a temple to Ba'al in Samaria and worshipped him. As if that was not enough, Ahab also set up an Asherah pole for worship of the goddess by the same name, which only further fanned the flames of apostasy among his people.

Jezebel was not only wicked, but she also was utterly domineering which is why Ahab submitted to her demands in all things religious. It was in her interest for Ahab to ignore God's commands entirely and become a pagan like her. She was a diabolical woman of forceful action. Almost without fail, whatever she ordered happened. When she spoke, people listened, that is, if they valued their lives.

When Elijah dared to challenge her prophets of Ba'al and then decisively proved them to be the frauds they were, subsequently killing them to rid Israel of their corrupting influence, Jezebel was outraged. She became determined to hunt him down and execute him like a common criminal.

She not only saw Elijah as a threat to her religion, but more important, as a threat to her authority. Like the true tyrant she was, she was not about to let his actions pass unscathed by her wrath. She didn't hesitate to bring the weight of the entire government down on Elijah's head, making him public enemy number one. As a fugitive, Elijah fled to the wilderness, safely away from the clutches of Jezebel. There he met with God who restored him from his pessimistic perspective of Israel's religious standing by reminding him that there were still seven thousand Israelites who had not bent their knees before Ba'al.

It's interesting that the Bible places Jezebel in the center of the conflict over Ba'al worship and Elijah's defeat of her prophets. In fact, even before the dramatic confrontation on Mt. Carmel, Elijah had told Ahab there would be neither dew nor rain for the next three years because of the spiritual condition of Israel. Ahab could have arrested him on the spot, but he didn't. Even though he hated Elijah's prophecies, he remained hesitant because he saw Elijah as a powerful prophet of God.

God instructed Elijah to withdraw eastward beyond the Jordan River, probably because Jezebel would have arrested him herself when she heard that the ensuing drought and subsequent famine was his doing. Then she would have tried to force him, by torture if need be, to bend to her will. Either that or have him executed like all the others.

Perhaps the best example of the difference between Ahab and Jezebel is found in the events around Naboth's vineyard, a beautiful piece of land that lay on the outskirts of Samaria, apparently within viewing distance from the palace (1 Kings 21). Because Ahab coveted that land, he went to Naboth the Jezreelite and offered to buy it or exchange it for another piece of land, which he described as "a better vineyard." Naboth respectfully declined the offer, citing the fact that the land had been owned by his family for generations, so he had no wish to sell the inheritance of his fathers.

Ahab then returned to his palace and in his petulant anger began to sulk over his inability to convince Naboth to sell his land to him. In his narcissistic world, Ahab was not used to being denied what he wanted. When Jezebel entered the room where she found him laying on his bed, sulking and refusing to eat, she demanded to know what was upsetting him. He told her about his conversation with Naboth and his refusal to give his land to him.

Jezebel was immediately disgusted with Ahab for being such a weakling, ordering him to snap out of it and stating she would take care of the problem. The writer of First Kings recorded her words this way: *"Jezebel his wife, said, 'Is this how you act as king over Israel? Get up and eat! Cheer up. I'll get you the vineyard of Naboth, the Jezreelite'"* (1 Kings 21: 7).

She had no real respect for her husband and he gave her little reason to have any. She saw his behavior as that of a petulant child throwing a tantrum over something he didn't like, instead of going after what he wanted. After all, that was her mindset. She let nothing get in the way of her own ruthlessness in obtaining whatever she put her mind to. She just couldn't understand someone who had the power he had as king, but didn't use it to force his will upon others. She was as malicious and unscrupulous as he was pathetically weak and self-centered. Together, they were an incomparable force for evil.

To implement her plan to steal the vineyard for Ahab, she sent letters in Ahab's name and with his seal to the noblemen of the city boldly revealing her scandalous strategy:

"Proclaim a day of fasting and seat Naboth in a prominent place among the people. But seat two scoundrels opposite him and have them testify that he has cursed both God and king. Then take him out and stone him to death" (1 Kings 21: 9). They did as she instructed (no doubt fearing for their own lives if they didn't), clearing the way for Ahab to march in and confiscate the land for himself. He didn't do any of the dirty work but was more than happy to take possession of the land. Whether he knew exactly how she pulled it off didn't matter to him (though I suspect he at least, knew it was done illegitimately). He had what he wanted and that's all that counted.

This amoral couple probably wouldn't have lasted together more than a few months had he not been king, which gave her the power, as queen, to live a life of luxury and control. Because Ahab no doubt knew her diabolical tendencies, he may very well have been afraid of crossing her. In any case, she was the mover and shaker in the family, even if she was pure evil in motion.

Ahab was no doubt strongly supportive of the marriage of their daughter Athalia to Jehoram, the son of Jehoshaphat, king of Judah. By drawing the Judahite king into his family as the father-in-law of his daughter, Ahab thought he had an automatic ally in case he had to go to war again to defend his nation against invasion.

Athalia was cut from her mother's cloth, strong-willed, contemptuous of others socially beneath her, and very controlling in her own right. Indeed, she and Jezebel had a tight relationship, which meant if Ahab wanted some favor from King Jehoshaphat, a godly king, he knew Athalia would be there in Judah's royal house to persuade him to bend to his will. And it wasn't long before that was precisely the case. After three years of peace between Aram and Israel, Ahab wanted to declare war against his longtime enemies so he could retake Ramoth-Gilead that he'd lost in previous wars.

Jehoshaphat was, at first, hesitant to join him as requested, wanting to hear first the advice from a prophet of God before taking any action. But even though the prophet Micaiah prophesied against Ahab and his plan to go to war, declaring it would be an utter disaster, Jehoshaphat decided to join forces with Ahab anyway. One cannot help but think that he felt obligated to do so because of his family connection to Ahab. From all appearances, it was a decision in which the presence of Athalia in Jehoshaphat's household advocating for her father was likely a major factor.

It would not be surprising if we learned that it was Jezebel's influence that was behind Ahab's sudden interest in becoming the aggressor in his relationship with the Arameans. It would have been just like her to urge Ahab to expand his kingdom east of the Jordan, which would have given them more regional power in an area to which they felt entitled. Besides, it was perfect revenge for everything their enemy had put them through over the years.

All his previous wars with Aram were largely defensive in nature when the Aramean king sought to rob Israel of its treasures. So, this about face was more than a bit suspect. Nevertheless, they were all pressed into war, one that proved every bit to be the disaster Micaiah had predicted.

In the end, Ahab died ignominiously in an ill-advised war of his own making and Jezebel died unceremoniously in a purge of the entire house of Ahab by Jehu. He was the commander of Ahab's troops stationed in Ramoth-Gilead and God had appointed him for the task. For two royals who repeatedly conducted themselves with violence, it seemed appropriate that they should die violently — only a slight variant of the axiom that those who live by the sword also die by the sword.

As ugly as the marriage of Ahab and Jezebel was, it serves as a prime example of what can go wrong when God is completely absent in the relationship. Exercising sheer naked power and silencing your opposition is bound to backfire sooner or later, not only with your enemies, as was the case with Ahab and Jezebel, but also with your friends and allies.

***

Points to Ponder

Every relationship, if it is to be vibrant, must necessarily draw its lifeblood from mutual respect and trust. Without those twin pillars of support, the relationship inevitably collapses into tolerance, at best, and utter disdain, at worst. Jezebel's marriage to Ahab represented both ends of that continuum. Whatever love there was at the beginning likely died along the way. She tolerated his immaturity and personal weakness as a leader only because she was unwilling to lose her power and wealth. But she also displayed uninhibited disdain for him, especially when he failed to act as ruthlessly as she thought a king in charge of his realm should act. She probably would have left him had he not been the ticket to her authority.

It's incumbent on every couple to periodically assess the current state of their marriage to determine if they relate to each other in ways that are perceived to be disrespectful or draw down on the level of trust in one another. Do you unwittingly hurt one another by certain habits of response or gestures of communication, which call for forgiveness and commitments to change? Are there areas of immaturity that are distressful to your partner but continue unaddressed? Is there ever any appearance of sarcasm or cynicism in your interactions together? If so, when does this occur?

Psychologist John Gottman and his research associate at the University of Washington have identified four things that reliably kill relationships, which he has euphemistically called, "The Four Horsemen of the Apocalypse"[4]. These include criticism, contempt, defensiveness, and stonewalling. In their studies, they have been able to predict divorce with 91% accuracy, a rather remarkable achievement. Though "the four horsemen" can poison the well, it's important to note, on the other hand,

---

[4] Cf., Gottman, John, and Silver, Nan, The Seven Principles for Making Marriage Work, Harmony Pub., 2015, pp.32-40, 45-51, 117, 163.

that conflicts per se are not a bad thing. To the contrary, they happen regularly in marriage, which is actually a good thing because they foster creativity and growth in a couple.

Conflict merely indicates that there are two individuals in the marriage, each with different tastes, different growing up experiences, different temperaments and personalities, and different habits built up over time. It should be expected, then, that conflicts would occur. They are a healthy part of the relationship, especially since they require negotiations that stretch us to change, adapt, and grow, not only as couples, but also as individuals. As Proverbs 27: 17 puts it, "Iron sharpens iron and one person sharpens another." What's not healthy is when we try to bury these differences.

The fact that diversity exists is evidence of the uniqueness of each marital partner, which is intended by God to be a bulwark against self-centered living. As we discussed elsewhere, conflict shouldn't be avoided, nor dismissed without the attention it deserves, but rather resolved with love and understanding. But the process of attempted resolution can go quickly off the rails and lead to disheartening damage to the relationship when the dysfunctional pasts of one or both of the partners are imported into the marriage. This is especially true when one or both spouses struggle with self-hatred or blistering self-criticism because of those pasts. Low self-esteem is ultimately the culprit in many fiery interactions among couples. It's what drives criticism of others and defensiveness in particular.

As opposed to positive criticism which speaks the truth in love about our weaknesses, Gottman and Silver focus on destructive criticism, which attacks the person rather than addressing the behavior. It's a species of criticism that assumes superiority for your own point of view while denigrating the value of your partner's perspective. As such, it is largely intended to demean and degrade your partner, which is judgmentalism at its worst. Contrary to the purpose of the tactic, placing the blame entirely on your spouse for a problem does not absolve you of culpability for your part in creating it.

If you add contempt and disgust to the mix, as was the case between Ahab and Jezebel, then the chances rise exponentially that the conflict will permanently damage the marriage. Contempt, which strips others of their dignity and attacks their integrity, is most often held when you focus exclusively on your spouse's shortcomings without giving any attention to your own. This lopsided perspective is what typically provides the false rationale for the self-righteous posturing of personal innocence. It's also the reason why your spouse will feel devalued and worthless in your eyes, which can, in the long run, be particularly devastating when he or she already struggles with issues of low self-esteem.

Many times people are not even aware they are coming across contemptuously. The slow eye roll, the strategic sighs, the pursed lips are all so well-ingrained that the individual is no longer aware that they're doing these things. They may even deny doing them. Instead, they see themselves as simply telling the truth — which means they're right and the other person is wrong — but they're frustrated that they can't seem to get that across without "unreasonable" opposition.

This commonly occurs in what I call, "historical accuracy arguments." These are arguments over different versions of events that have transpired in the past, recent or otherwise, in which memories differ over who did what to whom. American poet, Ogden Nash, had this to say to those tempted to endlessly argue every point: "Whenever you're wrong, admit it; whenever you're right, shut up!" That's good practical advice to anyone who is misguided enough to always seek the upper hand in conflict.

As this suggests, in most arguments, the reference point is invariably *the self*, which should tell you why you're unlikely to convince the other person of the "rightness" of your position. It should also tell you that what you're doing is probably sinful and perhaps terribly destructive to your marriage. It's sinful because it typically elevates the self as the source of infallible authority, a prideful position if there ever was one, and destructive because it usually attempts to either nullify or silence the other person, in effect canceling out their views. The seething resentment for being repeatedly shut down like that can eat away at the relationship like a corrosive acid.

In marriage, you must live with your spouse's weaknesses day in and day out, just as they must with yours. The truth is, it will never be the union of two perfect people, but with kindness, gentleness, and constantly offered forgiveness above all, you can successfully navigate the occasions of troubled waters by stepping outside your own view of self and making an honest attempt to see the world through your partner's eyes. Regardless of who's at fault, in the end, a happy marriage is, as American journalist and humorist, Robert Quillen once put it, "the union of two good forgivers."

Constantly blaming your spouse for one thing after another, while ignoring your own culpability, especially when you're expressing contempt for them as a person, are what most often speak to the level of defensiveness in your marriage. Yes, defensiveness can be aroused by *any* criticism, even the constructive type, in some people who have been hyper-sensitized by a dysfunctional home. But a lot of defensiveness in marriages is also the poisonous result of insensitive interactions within the relationship. That's why treating one another with respect is basic to reaching a satisfying conclusion in resolving conflict.

Stonewalling, the last of what Gottman and Silver describe as relationship-killing behaviors, is essentially a verbal, if not an emotional disengagement from the relationship altogether. It's the shut-down mode that puts an end to any substantive conversation. It frequently occurs after a long history of damaging interactions, which typically get their start in contentious families of origin, and then continue right into the marriage.

Stonewalling can be both an action and a reaction to a loss of trust in the relationship. Like hurling invectives intended to wound the other person, silence can be used as an aggressive weapon to inflict the pain on your spouse in retaliation to the perceived pain your spouse has inflicted on you. No one likes to be ignored; it tells them that you don't think they are even worthy to be heard. What's more, it neither displays love nor expects any in return.

On the other hand, stonewalling can be the defense of retreat to avoid further hurt. In this context, it's a passive reaction to conflict which telegraphs your rejection of any conflict at all. In such cases, you tend to see your spouse as a prosecuting attorney in the courtroom of marriage, one to whom you will always lose and can never win. Then, shutting down seems to be the only alternative if you want to remain intact emotionally when the storms hit.

Almost all the behaviors we've been discussing — the disrespect, the criticism, the contempt and disgust, the aggression, the passivity, even, on occasion, the retreat — were present in the marriage of Ahab and the over-controlling Jezebel. Unless you're weak, fearful, and insecure about your decisions, you normally don't like your life to be run by others. To be dominated like Ahab by Jezebel creates such an imbalance of power in the relationship that it only encourages contempt and withering criticism. In the world of matrimony, it is a deadly game that crushes any chance for a happy and fulfilling marriage.

Any marital bond that remains intact by the sheer force of circumstances can hardly be held up as a paragon of lasting joy. Nonetheless, you can learn from it which factors are important in making your own marriage last for the right reasons.

We have seen that this requires, with the help of the Holy Spirit, practicing the virtues of love without conditions, respect without judgmentalism, transparency without defensiveness, and disagreement without contempt. The greatest challenge for every believer is to live out these virtues when you're frustrated and feeling hurt and angry.

Remember, God doesn't expect us to be perfect, only that we be willing to learn to see our imperfect partner the same way He see us.

Part Four - Problem-Centered Marriages

Chapter 8

Hosea and Gomer: The Problem of Infidelity
Hosea 1-3:5

The prophet Hosea was called to minister to the northern kingdom of Israel in the latter half of the 8th Century BC during the reigns of the last seven kings of Israel, prior to its destruction by the Assyrians in 722 BC. By then, Israel's inhabitants were looking a lot like the idolatrous Canaanites whom Joshua had driven out centuries earlier. Underneath Hosea's prophecies of doom for a nation that had been called to serve the one true God but had forsaken its covenant and turned to other gods was always the promise of restoration.

This message was mirrored in his own marriage to the adulteress, Gomer, who proved to be persistently unfaithful to him. Some believe she had formerly been a temple prostitute at one of Ba'al's shrines. Others maintain that she was simply a sex-driven woman who couldn't keep her eyes from wandering. She was inherently unfaithful, much like Potiphar's wife who tried to seduce Joseph. Either way, when it came to promiscuous behavior, Gomer was hardcore.

In fact, her name was indicative of her behavior, since men would sate (gomer) their lusts with her. She was also identified as the daughter of Diblaim, a name derived from the Hebrew word *devalah*, meaning fig cake, which had a distinctly sweet taste, much like Gomer's words of enticement to the men she seduced.

As a promiscuous woman, Gomer would likely have been shunned by most law abiding Jews, perhaps even the subject of gossip and scandalous rumors. Before she was married, she probably had little or no means of financial support, which she could have used in her mind as an excuse to become a prostitute. As Hosea explained, Gomer said to herself, "I will go after my lovers who give me my food and my water, my wool and my linen, my oil and my drink" (Hos. 2: 5). Once Hosea came into the picture, she no longer needed to be concerned about those things, yet a life with a woman with that kind of background would be, at best, a cautionary tale of potential disaffection and regression into her old habits of promiscuity.

With those red flags staring him in the face, Hosea nevertheless purposely married this woman in obedience to God's command. He knew, of course, there was the risk that Gomer would be just as promiscuous as his wife as she had been before she met him. On the one hand, Hosea's marriage was intended to serve as a metaphor for the relationship between God and the nation of Israel. On the other, it meant that Hosea ran the danger of suffering heartache and humiliation as long as he was part of such a union.

It's tempting to think that Hosea quietly harbored the idea that perhaps he could win her over by his love and respect, despite her background. He may have already had strong rescuer tendencies, which God perhaps drew upon when He asked him to take on a marriage symbolic of His relationship with Israel. He knew that rescuers take their roles seriously, a fact which made Hosea a perfect candidate for such a purpose.

It's worth noting that a woman like Gomer could find a faithful, loving husband like Hosea, have children with him, and yet still find exclusive commitment to him almost impossible to maintain. She wasn't guilty merely of a one night stand that was a momentary slip into her former life. No, she was guilty of multiple affairs, even though she no longer needed the money, lived in a secure and nurturing home, and had the responsibilities of a mother to her children. It was obvious that nothing short of a miracle would stop her from indulging in her sexual addiction.

Of course, you can see the parallel of her life story and that of Israel's relationship with God, as unfaithful as the Jews were in following Him. These parallel narratives remind us of the serious consequences of the choices we make, as well as the paramount importance that forgiveness has in healing such a relationship. It's hard to miss the overwhelming impact of God's command in Hosea 3: 1 after Gomer's abandonment of the marriage in favor of further sexual affairs with other men: *"Go show your love to your wife again, though she is loved by another and is an adulteress. Love her as the Lord loves the Israelites, though they turn to other gods and love the sacred raisin cakes"* (which were apparently eaten in sacrificial feasts in the temples of Ba'al; emphasis added).

To ask Hosea to love Gomer as *the Lord loves the Israelites* was, at the very least, a tall task. It had to be supremely difficult for Hosea to do. After all, he had feelings, too. Having loved Gomer and faithfully provided a good home for her all those years, you can only imagine the level of betrayal he felt. Although he knew what her life was like before they were married, it's conceivable that he believed (or at least hoped) that they had turned the corner and that she finally saw the value of fidelity to one man. Alas, that was not the case.

Still, here was God telling him to go find her and show her his love once again, regardless of what she had done.

Notice God told Hosea to *show* her his love; in other words, behave towards her in a loving way, which was not necessarily what he was feeling inside at the moment. God knew that he was only human and would struggle to work up the emotional wherewithal to do what He asked. Yet He also knew that Hosea was an obedient servant, and by taking action on His command, His prophet could eventually change the narrative in his head.

Sometimes, acting your way into a new way of thinking can promote change faster than trying to think your way into a new way of acting. Just because you don't *feel* like doing something, doesn't mean you can't do it. In fact, we do that all the time. For example, you may not feel like going to the gym and doing some exercise, but that need not stop you from doing it. Indeed, after you're done, you're usually glad you went ahead and did it. Similarly, you may not feel like going to work on any given day, but you go anyway.

When you do something contrary to your attitudes, you're more likely to change the attitudes to conform to your behavior. This desire for consistency is called the need to reduce cognitive dissonance. The point is that whatever was going on inside Hosea at the time didn't have to interfere with going ahead and obeying God's command. And by acting in a loving manner toward Gomer, the chances were that Hosea's attitudes of disaffection with her affairs would turn to genuine forgiveness, which eventually it did.

If there was ever a more graphic occasion to experience the depth and breadth of God's love for fallen man, it was at this moment for Hosea. By reconciling with his wife after she had left him to sleep with other men, he discovered, no doubt to his surprise, that he could push through his pain and recover his love for Gomer. Acting his way into that mindset, rather than trying to think himself into it, proved to be quite effective for him.

Not only that, but in the process he also demonstrated prophetically the far greater love it would take for a wholly righteous God to reconcile with the people of Israel after enduring their degrading and adulterous betrayal through idolatry. His matchless love and endless grace are impossible to fathom without the help of some corollary human experience. For Hosea, reconciling with his wife after being so painfully abandoned by her gave him a unique perspective into the astonishing nature of God's benevolence toward Israel. It no doubt served to deepen his faith even further.

Sometimes, people ask why bad things happen to good people, but as the experience of Hosea demonstrated, valuable growth can happen as a result of them. God does not allow us to go through hard times without being there to teach us important lessons — either about Himself or about ourselves — if we are open to them.

When I had a bicycle accident a number of years ago that resulted in a fractured arm and a badly broken hip, it was a painful experience I wouldn't wish on anyone. It took extensive surgery and a long road of rehab to fully recover. At first, feeling pity for myself, I asked God, "Why me?" But later, after realizing that was a useless question, I asked God to teach me something from my injury. It was not long after that the doctors discovered I had a relatively rare hormonal disease that was slowly reducing the density of my bones. That explained why my injuries were so severe. The doctors told me it was a silent disease that is often not found until the person has become so osteoporotic that bones made brittle by its progression could break just by leaning over a handrail. By then, however, it's too late to reverse the effects of the disease.

Fortunately, there is medication that can arrest these effects if caught in time. My accident rang the alarm bells that directed my doctors to discover the problem. God had answered my prayer by teaching me that my accident revealed something I needed to know about my body. If you ask God for something, be prepared for an answer, although it may not always be what you expect.

Hosea had trained himself to be naturally attuned to God's desires, even during the tough times. Now, he was following God's directive to show his love to Gomer again. But before he could re-introduce her to his home, he first had to pay for the redemption of his wife who had essentially become a slave of her lover. It was reminiscent of a dowry which a groom used to give for his bride as a token of his love and commitment. According to Levitical law, Gomer could have been put to death as an adulterous wife (Lev. 20: 10), but she was offered restoration of her marriage in an act of exemplary grace.

No mention is made of Gomer's immediate response to Hosea when he found her and asked her to return home with him, other than her compliance to his request. The fact that she was apparently willing to return suggests that she realized her life with Hosea was good. She was loved and treated well, which was probably far better than what she got from any of the men who were primarily interested in her body, not her person. As Hosea put it, "*She will chase after her lovers, but not catch them...Then she will say, 'I will go back to my husband as at first, for then I will be better off than now'*" (Hos. 2: 7).

It's been said that if you want a marriage to last you treat it with the specialness it deserves. You don't let it become common or ordinary. Hosea's love was clearly extraordinary; despite her multiple affairs, which not only betrayed his trust but humiliated him before others, he persisted in his pursuit of her. He had chosen to love her. It's likely she was very surprised, even shocked, that he wanted her back after what she had done.

To be loved, accepted, and forgiven like that was undoubtedly alien to Gomer's experience, especially in a world where taking advantage of others was the norm. With her background, that would have been pretty much the only inducement that could have convinced her to return to married life.

Maybe she thought that her marriage was too good to be true, and sooner or later, he would turn her out like all the other men in her life had done after they got what they wanted from her. Leaving and having one affair after another would have ended the suspense. If that was the case, then when he tracked her down to retrieve her for his own, he proved that she was wrong, once and for all.

The story of Hosea is a beautiful metaphor of God's faithfulness to His promises and His love for His adulterous people. How many would have the grace God had to remain in a one-sided adulterous relationship like that? But for that reason, Hosea's reconciliation with Gomer prophesied the future return of the spiritual harlot — the nation of Israel — back to God. It also demonstrated that to Our Lord *no one* is beyond forgiveness and restoration.

If ever you begin to question God's love for you because life circumstances have dealt you a severe blow, you would do well to read the book of Hosea to regain your perspective.

Adultery, whether spiritual or physical, is one of those experiences in life that demands a heart of forgiveness. To many, that seems simply to be a bridge too far. To forgive someone who has deeply hurt you is, perhaps, the single hardest act of grace there is.

Yet Jesus gave His life for that very reason. How can we neglect so great a salvation?

***

Points to Ponder

The confirmation of an affair is almost always a devastating punch to the gut of the betrayed spouse who is first learning about it. After the initial shock, which occurs even in those who have had suspicions for a long time, a resident rage settles in that dwarfs the capacity to make wise decisions. What makes adulterous affairs so difficult to deal with is that they involve violations of intimacy, which goes to the very heart of personal lovability.

Betrayed spouses want to know why their partners felt they had to go outside their marriage to get what they wanted. In their bitter despair, they obsess over questions like, "Am I not enough for you?" or, "What does she (he) have that I don't have that would make you want to go behind my back like that?" They flood their conversations with a mixture of moral outrage and plaintive cries of deeply personal anguish.

They just can't get their heads around the fact that they've been so terribly betrayed, especially when they feel they haven't, to their knowledge, done anything wrong, or, at least nothing that would reach a level meriting rejection of their marriage. In their darker moments, they begin to turn on themselves. They'll start secretly questioning whether they're even worthy of someone's love. They may worry that others also will now see them as damaged goods. As anyone who has gone through this wrenching experience can attest, it can be immensely wounding to their self-esteem.

Hosea was dealing with a woman who had a history of sexual dalliances, mostly from her occupation as a prostitute. Obviously, he knew what he was getting into, even though he probably hoped for the best. Still, it's betrayal just the same and doesn't lessen the pain of discovering your wife has skipped out on you for another man. If there is no history of promiscuous behavior to begin with, as is often the case in Christian marriages, the shock becomes almost overwhelming.

If there's one thing Hosea repeatedly drives home it's that sin hidden in the shadows does not go undetected forever. Sooner or later it will be found out. Of course it's always known by God, but to others that discovery is sometimes accidental, or intentional at other times. It depends on the kind of affair your spouse has had. For it's important to understand that not all affairs are the same. Actually, there are five different types.

The first kind of affair is an "exit affair", when the offending spouse wants out of the marriage but doesn't want to be blamed for being the one who calls it quits. By having an affair and carelessly leaving clues to that effect, his or her spouse is likely to discover the tryst, accuse them of infidelity, and then, in a fit of rage, ask for a divorce. By acting like the victim of spousal rage and leaving the marriage, it becomes mission accomplished.

In marriage counseling, these can be detected early when one of the spouses is completely disengaged in the relationship and is apathetic. The exiting spouse has usually agreed to counseling only to prove that the marriage cannot be salvaged. It's not long before it becomes evident (to the counselor at least) that a third party is involved.

The second type of affair is the "revenge affair", in which the cheating spouse is angry over how he or she is treated in the marriage and has an affair to retaliate for the pain and suffering they've endured. You might think of it as giving your spouse a taste of their own medicine to make them realize they can't continue trifling with your feelings and get away with it without paying a price. It's the end result of long-simmering resentment that has continued unresolved. These people have trouble being honest to their spouses about what they feel in their marriage. Sometimes the marriage ends to the great despair of the offender, who may not have intended for things to go that far.

Third is the "attention-getting affair," which is more likely to occur when the offending spouse feels neglected or is taken for granted in the marriage; this, makes them vulnerable to the attentions of others. Essentially, the hidden motive behind the affair is to arouse jealousy in their partner and to let them know that they can be attractive to someone else.

There is a lot of loneliness in this kind of marriage, so they're also looking for companionship, which initially seems to be a rather benign motive. They typically refer to their lover as a close "friend" to remove the stigma of the relationship and to accuse their marital partner of being unreasonable if there is any protest about the amount of time they spend together.

A fourth type, the "stimulation affair", is more often found in those who see their marriages as having become boring, the product of numbing routine and no longer a center of interest. They are looking for something exciting, which usually means something clandestine or taboo. Essentially, the affair becomes an experimental testing of the waters to see what's possible outside their marriage. Sometimes you see this type of affair in people who dated few, if any, suitors before they met their spouse and wonder if they "missed out" by not playing the field more when they were younger. Of course this is built on a fantasy, but then so are all affairs in one way or another.

A fifth type, the "flattery affair", entered into by those who are not purposely going out and looking for someone else to fulfill their needs, but falling prey to the admiration of someone who is frequently complimenting them or seems willing to sit and listen to their problems and frustrations. Flattered by the attention, they succumb to the charms of their paramour.

It may mean that they're not getting these things sufficiently at home, though they're not necessarily aware of any major dissatisfaction at first. Unlike the other types of affairs, there is no intended message to the spouse. It's not uncommon, after the fact, that the offending partners realize, in horror, what damage they've done to their marriages and beg for forgiveness.

There are many nuanced variations of these main patterns, but they all have in common the same theme of idealization of the affair relationship. In other words, the lovers are typically idealized figures whose, positive attributes — those that are experienced in the manufactured world of their affair — have become the singular focus, to the complete exclusion of their negative attributes. This disproportionate attribution is what inevitably leads to the constant unfavorable comparisons they make to their spouses, which justify the logic of the affair in their own minds.

It's important to remember that such affairs do not really involve genuine love but are physical or emotional distractions from the unaddressed problems in their marriages. As one therapist put it, "The affair is a vacation, but not a real relationship. Once it becomes a real relationship with real-life realities, it ends." Statistics show that only a small number of them (roughly 5-7%) conclude with the two parties getting married. Of those, three quarters end up in another divorce. It's not hard to see why.

The relationship in an affair is normally built on quicksand, largely because it's nearly impossible to have the same level of trust in a person who has already violated a previous marital covenant. As the idealized image fades into the reality of the whole person, when disagreements and conflicts inevitably begin to surface, how can they know for sure that this person will not resort to infidelity as they did before? This is one of the major reasons why the few marriages that do emerge from affairs usually have a very short shelf-life.

Owning up to the responsibility of repairing a broken relationship after an affair is an incredibly difficult task, one that requires acceptance of incremental change, not a miraculous reunion. Like a three-legged stool, it must, at minimum, involve remorse, repentance, and contrition on the part of the cheating spouse.

Remorse is feeling deeply sorry for what you've done, while repentance is fully turning your behavior around, which also includes cutting off the affair completely. Contrition remains the hardest requirement because contrition involves acknowledging and accepting the natural consequences of your actions. And they can be many.

For one thing, it means being fully transparent about the affair and answering the nonstop blizzard of questions that are usually asked by a hurting spouse who is still trying to figure out how and why it happened. The offending spouse may respond by saying something like, "You've asked me those questions a million times. Don't you understand? I don't want to talk about this anymore; it's over and done with, so why rehash old news. Let it go, so we can move on."

If this is the case, then the third leg of the stool — true contrition — is missing and reconciliation will likely fail. Going through the gauntlet of questions is one of the first consequences of an exposed affair. Many others follow, including a rebuilding of trust that will take years, not weeks or months. If the cheating spouse doesn't have the patience or emotional stamina to accept these realities, then he or she doesn't grasp the impact their behavior has had on the marriage.

God has called us to be peaceable in our relationships with one another and that includes our marriages. Just as the cheating spouse must willingly submit to the unpleasantries that follow a disclosed affair, the offended spouse is called upon to consider the herculean act of forgiveness. Both must understand, however, that while trust is a matter of experience, forgiveness is an act of grace. Just as Hosea's choice to reconcile and to show Gomer his love again reflected God's grace in choosing to love and reconcile us to Himself, we also are challenged to do the same in our relationships.

Forgiveness does not mean naively dismissing the gravity of adultery, nor does it demand that victimized spouses take their wayward partners back. Jesus recognized this dilemma when He cited the exception of marital unfaithfulness when talking about divorce, even though God generally hates divorce. As Jesus taught His listeners, divorce became permissible only because of the hardness of men's hearts, but it was not that way in the beginning (Matt. 19: 4-9). Jesus was saying that divorces when the spouse has committed adultery and refuses to repent and turn away from a promiscuous life are permitted, even if they are regrettable.

In stating that divorce was permissible in cases of sexual immorality (Matt. 5: 32), He was by no means ruling out the importance of forgiveness, which is entirely separate from the disposition of the marriage. He understood that forgiveness is more for the forgiver than the forgiven. While it takes grace to make the conscious decision to release your feelings of anger, resentment, and vengeance toward someone who has hurt you, it also empowers you to acknowledge your pain without letting it define you. The Greek word for forgiveness means literally "to let go", like when you no longer demand payment for a debt owed to you.

Forgiveness is not "letting the offender off the hook", or, "letting him get away with his offense". It is especially not about playing the role of the victim, or even the martyr. Instead, it's a proactive choice that gives you peace of mind and frees you from the burden of unatoned rage and otherwise sliding inexorably into bitterness. It is sometimes said that bitterness is like drinking poison and expecting the other person to die. There is no doubt that it's corrosive to those who harbor it. Given enough time, bitterness will twist your mind and squeeze your character of every last drop of virtue. What's left, no one wants to be around.

When Jesus was teaching His followers to pray, He told them to ask for the forgiveness of their sins, but only if they meant it enough to forgive those who had wronged them. Otherwise, to ask for forgiveness that they themselves were not willing to give made a mockery of the request.

If we truly want mercy from Our Heavenly Father, how can we deny it to others?

Chapter 9

Ahaz and Abijah: The Problem of Being Unequally Yoked
2Kings 16; 18:1-8; 2Chron. 26:3-9; 28, 29:1-2

When a person of faith marries someone of either a different faith or no faith at all, they must be prepared for conflicts other couples don't have, conflicts which can create a lot of heartache. Questions about religious training of their children, what movies or other forms of entertainment are acceptable, moral conflicts over personal habits, and unpleasantries around church attendance or other similar events, are, to name a few, some of the topics, choices, and issues that can prove to be contentious in such homes.

Normally, believers are advised to stay away from serious dating or courtship relationships with those to whom they would be unequally yoked in terms of their faith. If you are already married to someone who doesn't share your faith, however, the advice is not to leave your disbelieving partner unless he or she demands that you either give up your faith or you give up your marriage (1 Cor. 7: 12-14). If the unbeliever decides to leave, the believer should not fight it, lest it create unnecessary quarrels and ill will: "A believing man or woman is not bound in such circumstances; God called us to live in peace" (1 Cor. 7: 15).

Given this basic teaching in the New Testament, let's see what we can learn by taking a look at an unequally yoked relationship in the Old Testament involving the struggles of a godly woman trapped in an ungodly marriage.

Although there are a number of such relationships from which we can draw an example, the marriage of Ahaz and Abijah is particularly instructive for women who are stuck in a dark relationship with a man whose actions are exceptionally blasphemous and morally bankrupt, yet he does not seem to turn against his wife in any notable way.

As queen, Abijah had a front row seat to witness her husband's unimaginable evil, yet she was unable to leave her marriage without creating a scandal that would have humiliated the king and endangered her. Besides, she still remained in a position to spiritually influence her son, Hezekiah, whom she knew would become king one day.

Judging from the fact that she was specifically called out as his mother (2Chron. 29:1), it appears that Abijah's primary focus had become her surviving son. As the daughter of Zechariah, the godly counselor to the popular King Uzziah who was, for the most part, faithful to the Lord (2 Chron. 26:3-5; 29:1), there is no reason to think that Abijah didn't live up to the Hebrew name her father had given her. Her name meant, "My father is Yahweh". In fact, according to Jewish sources, it was she who saved the young boy Hezekiah from the flames of the god Molech after Ahaz had previously sacrificed their eldest sons in pagan worship (2Chron. 28:3).

The name Zechariah was very common in ancient Israel, with 28 different characters in the Old Testament having the same name. Some were earnest followers of Yahweh and others were not. So, it shouldn't be surprising that the name has generated some confusion. In any case, by identifying Abijah's father Zechariah as the counselor to King Uzziah, everything else in the story makes sense, including the convenient marriage of Ahaz to the daughter of his grandfather's long-running spiritual advisor. It was convenient because it gave an air of legitimacy to Ahaz's throne it didn't deserve. This same Zechariah was very possibly the son of the God-fearing Jeberechiah, whom the prophet Isaiah (Isa, 8:2) took as a reliable witness of his prophecy against the Arameans and the northern Israelites, the enemies of Ahaz.

Although the family pedigree of Ahaz was a godly one, once Ahaz became king, he not only undid all the good his forefathers had done for the nation, but he became one of the most wicked kings ever to sit on the throne of Judah. Echoing the pagan backdrop of his sister state of Israel to the north, he made cast idols for worshipping the Ba'als, burned sacrifices of his sons in the infamous valley of Hinnom, where child sacrifice was conducted, and followed all the detestable practices of the Canaanites who had been driven out of the land by God's empowerment of the Israelites (2 Chron. 28: 1-4).

Because he had forsaken the Lord and caused his people to do the same, Ahaz met thunderous defeat at the hands of the Arameans, who took many of his people as prisoners and pillaged his treasury. He suffered heavy casualties in his battles against the army of Israel as well, having lost as many as 120 thousand soldiers in one day.

Instead of seeking God in his defeated condition, he sought the help of the pagan king of Assyria. Even when it was obvious that the hand of God had turned against him, Ahaz still refused to repent of his sin and turn back to Him. As the Chronicler put it, "In his time of trouble, King Ahaz became even more unfaithful to the Lord" (2 Chron. 28: 22).

He paid the price for that, too. Ahaz was shocked to receive a chilly reception from the Assyrian king when he visited him in Damascus to congratulate him for his victory over King Rezin and the Arameans. What he got in place of the expected embrace of allies was a stern order to begin paying a heavy tribute as a vassal state to the Assyrian empire, which only further depleted Judah's wealth.

We can only imagine what Abijah was going through during this time, watching her beloved people suffer under the brutal, godless reign of her husband, weeping helplessly over the sacrificial loss of her sons to the fires of Molech, and hearing the stories of Ahaz's immoral escapades with prostitutes as part of his idolatrous worship of Ba'al. Above all, she must have been sickened by his desecration of the Temple, inside of which he set up a pagan altar, moving the brazen altar aside to make accommodation for it. He even shut the doors of the Temple to the worship of Yahweh.

As we noted earlier, because of ancient Jewish custom, young women had little choice in whom they married. It was more often a family transaction than a courtship. To be fair to Zechariah, as advisor to King Uzziah, who did what was right in the eyes of the Lord, he may have expected that because Jotham, the king's God-fearing son, also became a good king, the line of godly men would simply continue with Ahaz, Jotham's son.

It's unlikely that anyone in the royal family anticipated the about-face Ahaz did. Certainly, they would not have endorsed the wholesale attack on the national worship of Yahweh, given their last century of rule. What was particularly disheartening was how readily the people of Judah took up the practice of idolatry again. Abijah found herself quickly surrounded by pagan courtiers with whom she had little in common in terms of her faith.

Zechariah had no doubt instructed his daughter to honor the Lord, just as he did with King Uzziah as his chief counselor. Now she was faced with having to live with Ahaz, a man who was systematically dismantling everything she and her father stood for, but without the power to do anything about it. If she had publicly protested, she would most likely have been executed, or at least banished from the palace, where she could no longer exert any further influence over her son Hezekiah. If that happened, Hezekiah could have headed down a very different path. So, Abijah wisely, even if sacrificially, decided to stay put.

There is no mention of the kinds of conversations Ahaz and Abijah had in their private quarters, nor, for that matter, was much said between them about matters of state at all. That's likely because Abijah had no real influence in the events of Ahaz's reign. What's more, their interactions were probably highly restrained by the volatility of Ahaz, particularly when things weren't going his way, which was often. We are told that, at the time of his travails with Kings Pekah and Rezin, he was also being attacked by the Edomites, who carried away prisoners of their own, and by marauding Philistines, who raided the Judean towns in the foothills and in the Negev. The enemies of Ahaz were coming from all directions, creating an unsustainable drain on Judah's resources. Sensing his weakness as a leader, they were going in for the kill.

Abijah undoubtedly understood these continuous attacks to be the result of God's displeasure with her husband, but she also knew that Ahaz was so set in his evil ways that he wasn't about to change. And she was right. As things went from bad to worse, he merely doubled down on his sin. Certainly she had no power to change his behavior. Her only recourse was to concentrate her attention on her son Hezekiah to prepare him to lead the nation of Judah in an entirely different direction, one that would hopefully restore the worship of the Lord as central to the life of her people.

When faced with such evil times, Abijah didn't give up and withdraw into her shell. Instead, she became proactive in training her attention to the task of raising her son to be a God-fearing man, like her father had instructed her. The only option she had was not to rise up in fruitless protest against her intractable husband, but rather to prepare for the day when his ruthless and corrupt reign came to an end. Clinging tenaciously to her faith, she was a model of courage in terms of what a spouse can do when all the other alternatives are closed to her.

Most likely, Abijah was identified as Hezekiah's mother in the Chronicler's description of his coronation because she was an important influence in his life even after he became king. From the very beginning of Hezekiah's reign, Abijah's efforts were richly rewarded. In the first month after he ascended the throne. He reopened the doors of the Temple, conducted the necessary repairs, dismantled the pagan altar, removed the idols, and summoned all the priests and Levites to announce that he was re-prioritizing the worship of the Lord. Among other things, he told the gathered assembly:

"Our ancestors were unfaithful and did what was evil in the sight of the Lord our God. They abandoned the Lord and his dwelling place; they turned their backs on him.....That is why the Lord's anger has fallen upon Judah and Jerusalem. He has made them an object of dread, horror, and ridicule, as you can see with your own eyes. Because of this, our fathers have been killed in battle, and our sons and daughters and wives have been captured" (2 Chron. 29: 6, 8-9).

You can almost hear the words Abijah whispered to him when he was a young boy growing up under her tutelage. She not only saved her son from the same fate as his father, but also she was instrumental in ultimately reshaping the policies of the nation. Instead of languishing in dispirited passivity, the quiet activism of her parenting succeeded in changing the history of her people. Her life showed that God can use even the most restrictive of conditions to further His purpose if only His people have the courage to make use of the opportunities they are given.

Did Abijah find her marriage to be happy and fulfilling? No. But, rather than clamoring for a divorce, which would have done nothing to make her life happier, she chose to find fulfillment in doing God's work in the life of her son. She knew that no matter what happened regarding the spiritual destiny of her husband, she could still raise her son to love the Lord and His statutes.

***

Points to Ponder

If Abijah had lived in the 1st Century AD as a believer in the early church, she may very well have been among those who posed the question to the Apostle Paul about whether or not she should divorce her pagan husband.

This was a particularly common problem in the early church where many of the women in their assemblies had been converted to the faith, but their husbands had not. Paul's answer was clear, if not always well received:

"If any brother has a wife who is not a believer and she is willing to live with him, he must not divorce her. And if a woman has a husband who is not a believer, and he is willing to live with her, she must not divorce him. For the unbelieving husband has been sanctified through his wife, and the unbelieving wife has been sanctified through her believing husband….How do you know wife whether you will save your husband? Or, how do you know, husband, whether you will save your wife" (1 Cor. 7: 12-14, 16).

It's apparent Paul viewed marriage as a potential means by which a disbelieving spouse might come to Christ. However, if the disbeliever refused to live peaceably with his or her believing spouse, then Paul argued that the believer was not bound in such circumstances.

In every question the Apostle addressed about marriage and divorce, the key to his response was the questioner's efforts to maintain fidelity to Christ and His teaching. If you could remain faithful within the confines of your marriage to an unbeliever, then for the sake of his or her soul, you were to stay in the marriage, even when you preferred not to have that burden. By telling them that each one should retain the place to which God had called them, Paul was saying that God would give them the strength to weather the mis-yoked, unequally-yoked condition on the possibility that it might lead to the entry of one more soul through the portal of heaven.

This is what God had done for Abijah, which enabled her to carry out the important task of saving Hezekiah from the evils of his father Ahaz. She wasn't able to turn her husband around, but she was given the grace of living to see her son elevated to the throne and begin carrying out the reforms she had wanted to see for so long. In her old age she also had the joy of getting to know her son's wife Hephzibah, who was a devout follower of God. To have the companionship of her daughter-in-law, and to witness the major changes in the religious life of her people as queen mother were fitting ways to close out her life.

If Abijah had had a choice in the matter, it's certain she would have sought a husband who was closely aligned with her faith. However, we don't know for sure whether Ahaz had abandoned his faith before he became king or whether that transformation occurred after he assumed power. In other words, it's not clear if he had shown his true colors before they married or not. Though it was probably prearranged, it seems doubtful that Zechariah would have given his blessing to their marriage if he had known what kind of man Ahaz would prove to be.

The lesson here is that your courtship is important not only in determining the quality of the person you're dating, but also the nature and quality of his or her faith. While some may dismiss the problem of being unequally-yoked with an unbeliever and think they can work things out if they run into conflict over it, Abijah's experience — though admittedly extreme — calls out the need to think twice before you make that decision. It can lead to anguish you never anticipated.

Too many marriages have been torn apart by this issue, either by the heartache of loneliness in the believing partner's faith or by arguments over the religious training of the children. Being in love with the person you marry is obviously important, but is not the only factor upon which you must base a decision to marry. To put it simply, love is not enough. Most couples are very much in love when they marry, but discover later that what they considered a disposable, resolvable issue has become a volatile conflict that has pushed their marriage to the brink of divorce.

The best time to explore these issues thoroughly is during courtship, not after. As mentioned earlier, most marriage partners acknowledge they were aware of the red flags in their relationship but had dismissed them as easily resolvable after they got married. They were reluctant to even discuss them in pre-marriage counseling for fear the counselor might advise them against getting married.

This kind of thinking is typical of an underlying insecurity about the relationship. Even the thought of possibly parting ways terrifies them. They sometimes treat the issue as if it's their last shot at the gold ring and that all would be lost if they looked at their relationship too closely. They want to live the fantasy because they can't bear the thought of losing the love of their betrothed.

In one such case, the counselor encountered some glaring problems he believed needed considerable time to explore in order to build better coping skills in dealing with some of their major differences. This couple had appeared to him to be quite immature in their lives, both separately and together as a couple. He suggested that they wait to get married until they had considered all the issues that represented challenges to their relationship.

They frowned at the suggestion, even though they had only been dating less than two months.

By the next scheduled session, they bounced into the room giddy with excitement—they had gotten married during the intervening weekend! Shortly thereafter, they ended counseling, thinking they could take it from there.

Six months later, the counselor received word that they had divorced. It was over the same issues they had refused to explore in pre-marriage counseling. One of those issues was the possibility that they would be unequally-yoked. His faith was clearly questionable while hers seemed genuine, though her walk was not well grounded.

After they got married, he seemed to lose interest in the relationship and began spending more and more of his time with his friends, most of whom he had met at bars. Soon there developed heated exchanges between them. She suggested they go to their pastor, but he was not up for that, having gone from sporadic attendance at church to dropping out entirely. She had continued to go on her own. It wasn't long before he came home and announced he was leaving her.

The tragedy of this case was that they were together long enough to have a child. She ended up bearing that child alone — he never even showed up for the birth. It became one more case of a child born into a single parent family.

Most marriage counselors will tell you that this scenario, or some variation of it, is more common than you would like to think. It is a sad epitaph on the contemporary culture of divorce.

If Abijah had one piece of advice to give to the modern world of marriage, it would most likely have been this: "Enter marriage with a sober eye on the faith of your partner. A mistaken impression here could consign you to a life of heartache and regret. Though I was not free to make that decision, you are. Please, don't abuse your freedom. The consequences are too great."

Coming from a woman who had seen it all, the good, the bad, and the ugly, such wise advice would be well-taken.

Part Five - Tender Marriages

Chapter 10

Jacob and Rachel: Putting Romance Back into Marriage
Genesis 28, 29, 30:1-22

Though the story of Jacob started out as a grim portrayal of deceit and subterfuge, it ended as a heart-warming story of unwavering love for a young woman who loved him back with equal fervor. It was the kind of marriage everyone yearns for, but few attain. It stood in stark contrast to Jacob's forced marriage to Leah, to whom he was not even physically attracted. As sad as that story was, his marriage to Rachel was a shining example of true intimacy and romance.

As described earlier in Chapter 3, Jacob colluded with his mother Rebekah, who favored him over his brother Esau, shortly before arriving in Haran, and cheated his older twin brother out of his father's blessing, fanning the flames of sibling rage. Now, he found himself living in his uncle's home as a refuge from Esau's threats to kill him.

Believing Jacob's life was in real danger, Rebekah had quickly made plans for his escape, telling him about Esau's intentions and urging him to flee to her brother Laban in Haran. She promised she would send word to him when all was clear for him to return. First she had to convince Isaac of the logic of her plan without revealing its real purpose.

To gain her husband's acceptance of the idea, she slyly used his disapproval of Esau's marriage to two Hittite women to make her pitch to send Jacob away from Canaan to family members living up north in the region of Aram to find a wife. Her subterfuge worked. Isaac readily agreed to the idea and summoned Jacob to inform him of the plan, commanding him not to look for a wife among the Canaanites:

> *"Do not marry a Canaanite woman. Go at once to Paddan Aram to the house of your mother's father Bethuel. Take a wife for yourself there from among the daughters of Laban, your mother's brother. May God Almighty bless you and make you fruitful and increase your numbers until you become a community of peoples. May he give you and your descendants the blessing given to Abraham so that you may take possession of the land where you now live as an alien, the land God gave to Abraham"* (Gen. 28: 2-4).

Succeeding in winning Isaac over to the plan, Rebekah gathered up Jacob's belongings and sent him northeast to the city of Haran, where her brother Laban lived, exactly as her husband had instructed. She hoped her son could stay there at least long enough for Esau's fury to subside, which might take months, if not longer. It turned out that Jacob lived with his uncle for more than twenty years.

During that time, he was introduced to Laban's two daughters, Leah and Rachel, who were both his cousins. He first met Rachel when he arrived at the outskirts of town in a field where local shepherds were watering their sheep. She was herding her father's sheep and arrived at the well to water them at the same time Jacob arrived. Immediately he offered to water her sheep for her, overjoyed that he had so fortuitously encountered a member of the family he was looking for. In short order, he informed her that he was the son of her father's sister Rebekkah. Rachel became so excited that she dropped everything she was doing and ran to tell her father. This was the first tangible evidence of her exuberance that was immediately appealing to Jacob.

When Laban heard of the arrival of his sister's son, he rushed out to meet Jacob and to usher him to his home. After having Jacob work alongside him for about a month, Laban decided that if Jacob was going to stay for awhile, he should pay him wages. So, he asked Jacob what he thought would be a fair wage.

By this time, Jacob had already fallen deeply in love with the younger Rachel, who was "lovely in form and beautiful", contrary to her less attractive older sister Leah, who was said to have "weak eyes". This likely meant she didn't have very lively or expressive eyes, or perhaps had pale eyes, possibly due to some form of opthalmia common among people living in that area.

The standards of beauty of that era put a premium on dark, expressive eyes that shone with a deep, almost luminescent luster.

Jacob surprised Laban with his response. Laban likely expected a proposal for a percentage of the livestock as payment, which was typical in that day. Instead, Jacob made a request for the hand of Rachel. He proposed that he work for Laban for seven years in return for his younger daughter. This was quite in line with the ancient Near Eastern custom of paying the father a "bride-price" for the privilege of marrying his daughter. Laban readily agreed to his terms, cryptically remarking, "Better you than some other man."

Once Jacob faithfully served his seven years to get Rachel — time that seemed to go by quickly "because of his love for her," — he went to Laban to collect his new bride. That kind of sustained commitment gave testimony to his passion and devotion to his betrothed.

That commitment was to be tested by the unexpected deceit of Laban, who switched daughters on him at the last possible moment, under the cover of dark. In the morning, when he saw Leah laying beside him, Jacob realized he had been duped. Angrily confronting Laban, he was given the lame excuse that the eldest daughter had to be married first. Laban told him if he really wanted Rachel, then he had to work for him another seven years.

As we saw earlier in Chapter 4, it was an act of cruelty, both to Jacob and to his own daughter, Leah, who was now consigned to a loveless marriage simply because it was a matter of convenience and profit for her father. Then again, Laban was not an honorable man. In fact, he continued to abuse Jacob's benevolence even after Jacob had completed his years of service to him. Jacob certainly could not be blamed for taking his wives, his servants, and his livestock and leaving Haran while Laban was away on business, which is exactly what he did.

From all indications, the glorious moment when he finally had his beloved Rachel by his side was the moment that made all the sacrifice of his labor, his endurance of injustice, and his determination to see it to the end worthwhile. True romance had finally made its mark in the family. Even the anger Jacob later displayed with Rachel over her being jealous of her sister's pregnancies did not originate from disgust or disillusionment, but from his sense of helplessness to do anything about her initially barren condition. It had nothing to do with how he felt toward her.

He loved her and wanted her to be content that she had an exclusive place in his heart. He wanted his love to be enough for her, though he understood the humiliation she felt over initially being unable to provide him with a child they could call their own. He was, like any Jew in the ancient world, keenly aware of the culturally-induced shame a woman felt when she couldn't get pregnant, believing it to be a curse from God. In fact, it was because of that very understanding that his heart was breaking for her. More than anything else, he simply wanted her to be happy, but there was nothing he could do about her infertility.

When she did have a child, whom they named Joseph, they both rejoiced over the occasion. Indeed, because of how much he adored her, he came to favor that child above all of his other sons, a reality that was a bitter pill for Leah to swallow and one the rest of his sons refused to accept. In time, Rachel bore him two children but she tragically died in childbirth with her second son Benjamin.

As described earlier, Jacob treated kindly but without passion his sons born to Leah and those born to the handmaidens of each wife. They were the progeny of women for whom he had no romantic attachment. In contrast, Jacob lavished love and attention on the sons he had by Rachel. Precisely because he was deeply in love with Joseph's mother, he embraced him at the outset with inordinate affection, which obviously did not go unnoticed by the others.

After Joseph disappeared when he was sold into slavery by his brothers, Jacob, unaware of their treachery, was inconsolable. They saw their father's interest in life shrink before their very eyes, a consequence which at last elicited compassion in his son Judah.

If you recall from that discussion, it appeared that the other sons of Jacob had finally figured out why Joseph had been favored. It wasn't something lacking in them; it was because Rachel was not their mother. It was unmistakably clear to everyone in the family that Rachel was the undisputed love of Jacob's life. Unfortunately, Leah knew that from the beginning.

They had finally realized from the pathetic shape their father Jacob was in that they had misinterpreted his motives. Their remorse set them up for the surprise of their lives. Soon enough they would learn of Joseph's true fate.

The favoritism spawned by the exclusivity of love between Jacob and Rachel created tremendous tensions and jealousies in a family which ended up having essentially three parents (or five, if you count the two maidservants Bilbah and Zilpah who each bore Jacob two sons). Such a complex family situation laid bare the critical role that unalloyed affection plays in the fulfillment of each person's deepest longing for attachment.

The obvious romance between Jacob and Rachel serves to remind us of the importance of loving our mates and keeping that love fresh. To Leah, as we saw in Chapter 4, it was soul-crushing because she had no hope of ever experiencing love like that. But at least it told her sons not to merely "settle" for a mate because social convention dictated it, but rather to seek the hand of a woman they truly loved. Only then would their marriages be something more that merely a means for procreation for the sake of posterity.

After Rachel had given birth to Joseph, Jacob wanted out of Haran and away from the manipulative influence of his father-in-law. Now that he had the son he always wanted by the love of his life, he didn't want his wife (or his sons) to be cast under Laban's religious spell any longer. Remember that it was only after they separated from Laban and the pagan worship that surrounded him, that Jacob was free to have his wives rid themselves of their household idols and devote themselves fully to the worship of the Lord.

Even after twenty years of life in a pagan culture, Jacob was still faithful to his God. It's not a stretch to believe that his love for Rachel and their son Joseph was a major factor in his decision to leave Laban behind and forge a new life somewhere else, where he could immerse his family in the faith of his fathers. The purity of his love for Rachel had prompted a cleansing from any influence the impurity of idol worship might have had on them if they had stayed.

This is essentially what happened in Babylon over a millennium later when the Jews rediscovered their zeal for God and shook off the chains of their idolatry. The result was to increase their desire to leave behind the pagan culture of their Babylonian captivity and start over once again in the land of Canaan as a people under God's rule. With a stronger loyalty to their Lord came greater resistance to foreign religious entanglements, though the degree of their obedience to God's statutes still remained far from what God desired of His people. In fact, as time went on, the unfaithfulness of the people and their priests grew to the point of later rebuke by God's prophets (e.g., Malachi 1:6-2:9; 2:10-16). Their love for God needed constant rejuvenation or else they slipped back into practices that were dishonoring to Him.

This tendency for their love for the Lord to cool over time applies to loving one another as well. We see that true conjugal love likewise requires tireless effort and unflagging devotion. There must be a desire to bathe it in the cleansing power of commitment, which includes centering it on the spotless character of God's love. It's in the interest of the purity of our love that we seek to free ourselves from anything negatively impacting our marriages and embrace every practice that is in conformity to our faith.

This is the marital equivalent of seeking first the kingdom of God and His righteousness (Matt. 6: 33). This is what Jacob and Rachel did in walking away from the idolatrous Laban and his city of Haran to establish their own identity in God in the land of His promise. It's the first spiritual step you can take to anchor your marriage in the bedrock of obedience to His commands.

The powerful romance between Jacob and Rachel, which continued to be cultivated throughout their marriage, provided the incentive to always aim high for their relationship. It was because they had so integrated their passion for one another into their dedication to God that their relationship was blessed with a son who became an eventual healing force in the family. These events not only shaped the future of their immediate family, but also the ultimate future of the nation of Israel.

Such was the pivotal moment in redemptive history that preserved the fulfillment of the Abrahamic covenant, from which would eventually come the new covenant in Christ. Indeed, the gracious and unselfish nature of Jacob's marriage to Rachel, together with the devotion and affection of their commitment, give us a human corollary of the kind of covenantal love offered to us through Jesus.

***

Points to Ponder

It might surprise you how often people mistake initial infatuation for the evidence of true love. Both involve romantic feelings and at first both give at least, a wide berth to imperfections, mostly by producing blindness to them. What's more, early romantic feelings greatly elevate your mood; in some cases, to the point of ecstasy. Contrary to infatuation, which is an inch deep and a mile wide, true love endures great adversity. It weathers setbacks and disagreements. It even survives the volatility of emotions when conflicts and misunderstandings occur.

Infatuation, on the other hand, is like a wisp of steam that lingers for a moment in the air and then disappears. It's built on the quicksand of rapid emotional reactions that are, in reality, a product of wish fulfillment in lieu of adequate knowledge of the other person. Like all fantasies, it begins dissolving the moment partners encounter hardship and difficulties.

Contrary to the message contemporary culture gives you, the absence of love is not hatred. It is apathy. It is the lack of commitment and willingness to work for the relationship. It's the disinterest of the disengaged observer. It's looking for excuses to dismiss your partner's motives, to casually assume the worst rather than assume the best. It's finding reasons to spend more time apart and minimizing time together.

The slow but steady transformation of culture has been insidious in undermining the reasons for staying together. The culture-shaping elites, without skipping so much as a single beat, rationalize betrayal and normalize remarriage. They frame intimate relationships as nothing more than experiments in determining compatibility. They tend to paint single-parent families as equally healthy as two-parent families for the children in them. They portray relationship anomalies and gender aberrations as merely alternative ways of finding happiness.

The worst part is that these new aphorisms are couched in a cynically crafted piety designed to slip toxic ideas by the dozing censors of the minds of ordinary people dazed by the acceleration of change. Is it any wonder that the unacceptable divorce rate is largely ignored, or that we're seeing a general devaluation of the institution of marriage itself, even by those who are charged to protect it?

The result of all this is an increasing inability to make lasting attachments that mean anything. Commitments have become lighter than air. The sanctity of intimate love is being reduced to obsolescence. There is a rising doubt about both, even though they constitute the meaning for which we were created. The kind of love that Jacob and Rachel enjoyed seems to modern secular society more like a fable than a reality to be achieved; it seems a pale shadow of the simpler life of times past, rather than the nuanced, complex life of contemporary living.

To the Christian, however, the marriage of Jacob and Rachel represents the God-given capacity to love deeply and to resurrect the vanishing common ground of devotion to one another by keeping alive the flame of passion and romance. To value what your partner values, not necessarily because of the thing valued, but because you love the person doing the valuing, is a characteristic of true romantic attachment. Its promise of unity is rooted in the appreciation of diversity.

This is but another advertisement for the integrity of the covenant between two people who have pledged their fidelity to one another. It's something that secular culture finds difficult, if not impossible, to reproduce, mainly because it lacks the stamina for making choices that reach much beyond the perimeter of whim.

Such cultural thinking misses the point that abiding romance in marriage is what waters the parched soil of a relationship otherwise caught up in the dust of routine and habit. Instead, modern culture sees romance as an intense, but short-lived passion, an exciting phase that precedes the routines of marriage, but then vanishes with the more mundane reality of togetherness worn thin.

That's why modern man is no longer shocked by multiple flings which attempt to pacify an addiction to momentary passion. In fact, the film industry glorifies this obsession. To our contemporaries, romance is almost always transitional, and rarely trans-situational. Any degree of permanence is unexpected, which is why we have dwindling statistics for long-lasting marriages.

Romance is not the tacky scene of some Hollywood movie. It is the studied purpose of making precious the thoughts and feelings of your chosen life companion. It was Jacob's penchant for making everything special about Rachel, including the children she bore him. Indeed, after her death, he clung tightly to those children as the only living vestige of Rachel's sanctifying presence. Romance is evident in the gentle hands of both husband and wife, which mold and shape the clay of marriage into something of beauty and splendor, something worthy of admiration.

When Scripture describes Jesus' relationship with the church, it conjures up the image of the love of the Groom for his Bride. The intensity of His attachment, His desire for intimate connection, and, yes, even the romance of courtship with His beloved are all bound up in the notion of His unparalleled love for us. If the purpose of His love is to inform ours for one another, then the element of romance is indispensible to our marital commitments.

Certainly, Jacob and Rachel would have had no trouble saying "Amen" to that.

Chapter 11

Boaz and Ruth: Love and Selfless Responsibility
Book of Ruth, Chaps. 1-4

Like the story of Jacob and Rachel, the courtship and marriage of Boaz and Ruth involved plenty of romance intermingled with tense, uncertain moments before their happy union. Their story, however, started from the roots of tragedy, agonizing grief, and the collective despair of three women.

Ruth was a Moabite woman who had married one of Naomi's sons, Mahlon; her fellow Moabite, Orpah, became the wife of Naomi's other son Kilion. When there was a severe famine in the land, Naomi and her husband, Elimelech had moved from Bethlehem to Moab in search of a living there.

Shortly thereafter, both of their sons had married and they all settled down together with dreams of a bright future. However, it wasn't long before Elimelech unexpectedly died, leaving Naomi a widow while still relatively young. This tragic event was followed within a decade by the loss of both of her sons as well. It was no surprise that Naomi was in a state of utter despair, as were her two daughters-in-law who had now also become widows.

Alone, deeply depressed, living in a foreign land far from any kinsfolk who could rally to her side, and learning that Judea had recovered from its famine, Naomi decided to return home where she could be surrounded by family and friends. She informed her two daughters-in-law of her plans and urged them to return to their families where they could start life over again. While Orpah only reluctantly agreed, Ruth was adamant about going with Naomi, despite the risks it meant for her and in spite of Naomi's loving arguments to the contrary. Such was the powerful love Ruth had for her mother-in-law.

The two of them moved back to Bethlehem, familiar territory for Naomi, where she still had some friends who would welcome her... But Ruth was now the foreigner, subject to the prejudices of the local inhabitants who viewed the Moabites as their enemies.

Being the much younger of the two, Ruth was determined to help get Naomi back on her feet financially by going out to the farms nearby and joining those who gleaned the fields for survival. Large grain farmers allowed those who were poor to follow after their harvesters and pick up — glean — the missed grain for themselves. Ruth, the outsider, risked poor treatment, which Naomi cautioned her about, urging her to be careful. As it turned out, she found herself working in a field belonging to Boaz; unknown to her, he was a relative of Naomi's on her husband's side from the clan of Elimelech.

When Boaz arrived at the end of the day to see how harvesting was going, he immediately noticed Ruth, an unfamiliar face which instantly caught his attention, both for her beauty and for her apparent work ethic as he watched her laboring behind his harvesters. He asked his foreman who she was, and he replied, "She is the Moabitess who came back from Moab with Naomi." indicating that he had allowed her to glean with the others because of her relationship to someone he knew who happened to be related to his boss. He confirmed her tireless industry when he added that she had worked steadily from morning until evening with only a short break in between. Obviously, he was impressed….and so was Boaz.

Boaz then went over to Ruth, and after introducing himself, told her he wanted her to glean exclusively in his fields and that he instructed his men not to hassle her, but to leave her alone to do her work. What's more, he urged her to drink freely from the water jars that were made available to the others whenever she felt thirsty.

Ruth was taken aback. Dumbfounded that she had found such favor in the eyes of the owner of the fields, she asked Boaz why he was being so kind to a stranger like her, and a foreigner from a hostile land no less. His reply stunned her:

> *"I've been told all about what you have done for your mother-in-law since the death of your husband—how you left your father and mother and your homeland and came to live with a people you did not know before. May the Lord repay you for what you*

have done. May you be richly be rewarded by the Lord God of Israel, under whose wings you have come to take refuge" (Ruth 2: 11-12).

Boaz later quietly arranged it with his harvesters to leave some extra stalks of wheat for Ruth to ensure her success at gleaning. When Ruth returned home bringing her unusually large amount of grain to Naomi, she told her everything that had happened. Naomi was especially delighted to learn that Ruth had worked the fields owned by Boaz, her close relative, whom she identified as one of her "kinsman-redeemers".

After some time had passed, Ruth was becoming a fixture among the servant girls of Boaz and a favored one at that. Naomi, convinced that Boaz was attracted to Ruth, decided to play matchmaker. She encouraged Ruth to make a bold move by going to the threshing floor in the evening and, after Boaz finished his work and had eaten, when he lay laid down to sleep, to uncover his feet and lie down next to him. Though someone else might have taken advantage of her while they were alone on the threshing floor, Naomi was confident that he would act responsibly.

Already recognized as a woman of noble character, Ruth took actions that could only be interpreted as an unspoken request for marriage. In other words, she was announcing the fact that she had fallen in love with him and was asking him if he was interested in her, too. In doing so, she was appealing to Boaz's kinsman obligation as a provision of a levirate marriage, a custom in which the nearest relative of the deceased would marry his widow in order to continue his posterity.

The fact that she followed her mother-in-law's instructions to the last detail told Naomi what she already suspected, namely that Ruth was deeply attracted to Boaz. By calling on his responsibility as a kinsman, she was actually hoping underneath that he would return her love. Ironically, it was Ruth's sense of responsibility to take care of her mother-in-law who had lost everything that first attracted Boaz.

As she had hoped, Boaz did not reject her proposal, but, instead, immediately blessed her, commending her for her "act of kindness", by which he meant refraining from going after a younger man. Seeing her through the lens of his love for her, he apparently thought she was so attractive that she could have had almost any man she wanted. It served to only increase his esteem of her to be "willing" to marry an older man in order to follow through with her commitment to her deceased husband. Of course he wanted her, but he didn't think he had a chance with her given their age difference and given that she would be a great catch for anyone, including those he considered to have more to offer than he.

Now that he knew her intentions, he more than happily accepted the responsibility of being her kinsman-redeemer, but he first had to check out a closer kinsman who, according to levirate law, had the first right of refusal. Once that hurdle was crossed, the way would be cleared for him to marry Ruth. Regardless of that hiccup in the plan, Ruth knew her love had been reciprocated, and that's what counted to her. Now, her only prayer was that this other kinsman was not interested in becoming her kinsman-redeemer.

The very next day, when he met with that kinsman, Boaz was determined to present the issue in terms that would be difficult for him to accept. At first, he told him that Naomi was trying to sell some property, and, because he was the closest relative of Naomi's, asked him if he was interested in redeeming it to keep the property in the family. He readily agreed to that proposition until he heard the second part of the deal.

That's when Boaz informed him that Ruth, the Moabitess, as well as Naomi, were part of that settlement, since, upon the death of Elimelech the ownership of the land passed to his son, Mahlon, and, as a result of his death, passed to his widow Ruth. According to levirate law, that would obligate him to also take Ruth as his wife in the bargain.

This kinsman hadn't seen Ruth, but it didn't matter. He knew that she was young enough that he could very well have a child by her, in which case, that child would not only inherit the property in question, but possibly part of his estate, too. That had not been a problem with Naomi, who was well past child-bearing age. There is no mention of children that he might have already had to whom his own property would pass. Perhaps, he didn't want to take the chance, especially since Ruth was a Moabitess, not a Jewess. Inasmuch as Moab had been an enemy of Israel in the past, most Bethlehemites were prejudiced against them.

Boaz knew all these things, which is why he presented the situation as he did, including his specific mention that Ruth was a Moabite woman. Without hesitation, the kinsman rejected the offer, calmly ceding his rights to Boaz. At last, Boaz was free to marry the woman he loved, but had not previously dared to think she could ever be attracted to him. It must have been an indescribable moment for him.

He turned to the assembled tribal elders who were serving as witnesses to the transaction and proudly declared:

"Today you are witnesses that I have bought from Naomi all the property of Elimelech, Kilion, and Mahlon. I have also acquired Ruth the Moabitess, Mahlon's widow, as my wife, in order to maintain the name of the dead with his property, so that his name shall not disappear from among his family or from the town records. Today you are witnesses!" (Ruth 4: 9-10).

His declaration formally included the entire agreement, but the only part that was of true interest to Boaz was the announcement of his marriage to Ruth. The elders heartily congratulated him and wished him well.

Returning to Ruth, he told her all that happened and joyfully proclaimed they were to be married. So, she became the wife of Boaz and together they produced a son whom they named Obed.

That boy was privileged to grow up in a very happy home, which included his doting grandmother, Naomi, who was more than thrilled to babysit him whenever they needed her. So attached was Naomi to the child that her friends said that "Naomi has a son!"

It was only fitting, then, that Obed became the father of Jesse and the grandfather of King David in the ancestral line of the Messiah.

What started as mutual admiration of one another for the noble character each displayed ended in a budding love that transformed the lives of them both. Ruth had been deeply impressed with the uncommon kindness Boaz had shown her as a stranger and as a foreigner whom many Jews would have treated harshly.

What's more, she thought highly of the way Boaz conducted himself with his harvesters and with the servant girls, treating them each with great respect and dignity. It was the kind of gentle authority that anyone would hold in high regard, especially the servant girls who often found that sparingly, if at all, in other areas of their lives.

Likewise, Boaz had been impressed by the sacrificial love Ruth had shown to Naomi, and her willingness to take on the responsibilities of caring and providing for her, even though that was not normally the job of a daughter-in-law. He knew few women would have done the same in her situation. He was also struck by her indefatigable work ethic and beguiled by her beauty. He could not help but notice her every move. Yet, he never let on that he felt anything other than the respect he seemed to show everyone else, perhaps, because he was fearful he might embarrass himself if he revealed his growing attachment to her.

Respect is the first foundational stone to be laid in any healthy marriage. Boaz and Ruth illustrated that age difference was not as important as devotion and honor as qualities of a relationship. Taking your love for your spouse seriously means also taking your responsibility to meet his or her needs seriously. That starts with understanding what those needs are. Each partner of this biblical couple was the kind of person who listened carefully to what others said and spoke only after they had gained understanding. And both were immensely loyal in their attachments.

If you contend that these are important attributes of a happy marriage, then you will get no argument from Boaz and Ruth!

***

Points to Ponder

In today's culture, the exclusive responsibilities of marriage have increasingly been taken more lightly, largely because the institution of marriage itself has declined in stature as a source of fulfillment. Societal trends in redefining marriage, growing secularization of the populace, the advent of political correctness, and fundamental changes in gender roles, and even in gender identity itself, have all contributed to a weakening of the commitments that marriage requires. This reality can be seen in the abysmal divorce rates, the prevalence of single parent families, the skyrocketing rise in co-habitation, and the alarming statistics of spousal abuse and child abuse and neglect.

Even among Christians who are active in their churches, the divorce rates are unacceptably high, although, contrary to earlier claims, they are still significantly lower than non-churchgoers. Nominal Christians — those who call themselves Christians but aren't actively engaged with their faith — are actually *more likely* to get divorced than the general population. It seems that their lack of commitment to their faith is mirrored by their lack of commitment to their marriages. If they aren't authentic about what they believe, they're not likely to be authentic about their relationships either.

With so many factors tearing at the fabric of marriage, it is all the more important that the Christian community re-examine its dedication to the attributes of a lasting and fulfilling marriage, attributes which begin with our covenantal relationship with God. That covenant not only carries with it the joy of access to God's eternal presence, but also the responsibility of reaching out beyond ourselves and selflessly loving others. Boaz and Ruth understood this responsibility to include the devotion and honor they accorded one another in the God-given enterprise of marriage.

Passion and romance do not merely stop at the shore of love-making. They are designed to permeate every responsibility you have as a husband or wife to nurture peace and kindness in your relationship. The Apostle Peter noted that people can be won over to the faith simply by the purity and reverence of your lives (1Peter 3: 1-2). He continues on to describe the secret of beauty for women to their husbands and the secret of true leadership of men to their wives:

> *"Your beauty should not come from outward adornment...Instead, it should be that of your inner self, the unfading beauty of a gentle and quiet spirit, which is of great worth in God's sight. For this is the way the holy women of the past who put their hope in God, used to make themselves beautiful......Husbands, in the same way, be considerate as you live with your wives, and treat them with respect as the weaker partner and as heirs with you of the gracious gift of life, so that nothing will hinder your prayers"* (1 Peter 3: 3-7).

By "weaker partner" Peter did *not* mean more emotionally fragile or helpless, as some mistakenly believe. Rather, he meant the obvious reality of physical strength which reflects the difference between men and women in their levels of testosterone. To put it simply: Men are physically stronger that women. Actually, in this particular passage, the apostle was cautioning men never to use their superior physical strength to intimidate, dominate, frighten or otherwise do violence to their wives, but instead to treat them with great kindness and thoughtful regard. Indeed, Peter's letter is the most direct teaching against spousal abuse in the entire New Testament.

Boaz and Ruth would have perfectly understood Peter's teaching. It was their overwhelming kindness and respect toward each other that triggered their initial attraction to one another. Even in their world, where culture was male-dominated and where women had few rights, they realized the importance of character in marriage, in which taking responsibility for nurturing your partner was a priority. That it involved mutual submission was intuitively implied.

"Submission" is often a hot-button issue, particularly in the feminist era. But it need not be, since its biblical meaning is routinely misconstrued. Above all, it does not mean becoming a doormat; nor does it suggest self-abnegation as an ideal. Neither does it signal that one becomes a puppet and the other a puppeteer. Instead, it means the humility of putting your spouse's needs ahead of your own. The greatest impediment to a fulfilling marriage is the problem of selfishness.

When Jesus spoke of divorce, He said it was only made necessary because of the hardness of our hearts. That hardness that He spoke of was the selfishness that distances us from God's design for true intimacy. When He said that it was not that way in the beginning, He meant that man was not created to be selfish; it was sin that twisted the human soul into its misshapen form, unrecognizable in its purpose and corrupted by its obsession with the self.

From that moment on, every relationship was permanently stained with the power struggle for ascendency. Only then did the contest determining who controls whom become a staple of human interaction, both within the family and in the public sphere. Marriage was merely its most intimate casualty.

But isn't it true, as some argue, that the Bible teaches the husband is the head of the wife, therefore, giving him authority over her, so that all final decisions reside with him? Isn't it the wife who must submit to her husband in everything?

This question arises from disputes over the Apostle Paul's discussion of marriage in his letter to the Ephesians. What's left out of the argument implied by this question is the second half of Paul's statement. He declared that the husband is the head of the wife *as Christ is the head of the church*. So, the question to ask is how was Christ the head of the church? The answer to this can be found in Jesus' interaction with the disciples concerning the dispute among them about which one of them was considered to be the greatest, as petty as that clash was.

Jesus responded to them with the declaration that the greatest among them should be like the youngest, which would have been the one whom they considered the least qualified. To underline His point, He added that the greatest should also rule like the one who serves. Then He illustrated this with a simple question, the answer to which was so obvious that He answered it himself:

> *"For who is greater, the one who sits at the table or the one who serves? Is it not the one who sits at the table? But I am among you as one who serves"* (Luke 22: 27).

Everyone knew, of course, that the one who sits at the table was the master of the house and, therefore, greater than the bond servant who served him. Yet, here was their Master telling them He identified with the servant, not the one being served. What He was saying was that if your aim is to be the greatest, then use God's measurement for greatness: First and foremost, have the humility to serve others. That means putting their needs before your own.

Jesus was the head of the church precisely because He held nothing back, selflessly serving her unto His death. He knew that our redemption and consequently our peace depended on His sacrifice. The Apostle Paul picked up on this teaching to inform his Ephesian audience, who lived in a city that reveled in selfish pursuits, that the husband's role is sacrificial like that of Christ's with the church.

Paul followed this with the further clarification that the husband was to love his wife exactly like Christ loved the church: Submissively, thoroughly, sacrificially, wholeheartedly, sincerely, authentically, comprehensively, with nothing held back. It means serving his wife's needs without the hidden agenda of expecting something back.

When confronted with the leadership of selfless love, the wife is asked to reciprocate that service in her submission to him, which, if such conditions exist, Paul predicted she will joyfully do. So, Paul outlines the two sides of submission given to the husband and his wife that will issue forth in a happy, fulfilling marriage. The trouble is the selfish heart wants to upset this balance, and, indeed, many times it does. But that doesn't deny the efficacy of the design.

Just as your faith is a growing life attachment to your God, so also must your love reflect a growing life attachment to your mate. That can only happen if you succeed in defeating the enemy of selfishness that destroys it all.

No better example can be given of such a triumph than the marriage of Boaz and Ruth.

Chapter 12

Elkanah and Hannah: The Significance of Compassion
1Samuel 1-4

Sometimes we meet a couple in the Scriptures, not because of who they are, but because of what they did that profoundly affected the national life of Israel. Such was the case with Elkanah and Hannah, the father and mother of the priest and prophet, Samuel, who was a key figure during the transition from the period of the Judges to the period of Israel's monarchal kingdom. Their story spans the first two chapters of 1 Samuel.

Elkanah was a Kohathite Levite. He was also the great grandfather of Heman, who served with one of the Levitical clans that contributed musicians appointed by King David to supply the music for the Tabernacle, the Tent of Meeting, until Solomon built the Temple of the Lord in Jerusalem (1 Chron. 6: 31-32).

In what seems, at first glance, like a contradiction in the 1 Samuel passage, Elkanah was also described as an Ephraimite, which, as some have argued, would appear to have ruled him out of the Levitical line. Others argue, however, that given the context, it's much more likely that the term "Ephraimite" that is used in 1 Samuel 1: 1 referred to his place of residence, not to his lineage.

This is, I think, the best interpretation, especially since the verse specifically tells us that Elkanah lived with his wife in the hill country of

Ephraim. Besides, it was quite common for unneeded Levites to travel all over Israel during the time of the Judges, performing some of their duties outside of the Tabernacle (e.g., Judges 17: 7-13). So, there is no need to posit a contradiction when there is already good evidence of an alternative explanation.

From the different clans of Levites who served as religious officials, it was exclusively the Kohathite clan that provided the Aaronic priests to serve in the Temple. This gave men like Elkannah greater significance to their communities because of their reputation as having sterling character. Certainly, Elkannah was one who lived up to that reputation.

We are told that Elkanah had two wives, one named Hannah and the other, Peninnah. Hannah, his first wife, was barren, while Peninnah had children. This suggests the "primary-secondary wife" custom had come into play. If you recall, this cultural custom required a wife who couldn't bear children for her husband to supply a handmaiden as a proxy wife to ensure his posterity. It was the same custom that supplied Abraham with Hagar as his proxy wife when Sarah was barren, and with pretty much the same results.

Like Hagar, Peninnah constantly harassed Hannah about her inability to have children, provoking her to tears on numerous occasions. It seems that many of these so-called proxy wives felt inferior from the start because they knew full well that they had not been specially chosen by a man but were serving merely as back-ups that were needed for procreation and nothing more.

So, they used their fertility as a badge of achievement to boast to their mistresses because they believed they had nothing else of significance to offer in life. Employed concubines, which is what they really were considered, were little more than servant girls doing their culturally-approved duty.

Is it any wonder that this arrangement, though common in the day, was not God's desire? He knew what this sinful practice tended to produce. Of course, He knew that men were creatures of their culture, who saw such a practice as properly normative in view of the importance of posterity, instead of understanding it as the sin that it was. Nevertheless, it was inevitable that the contempt of rivalry and the reactionary jealousy over vying for the husband's attention would begin to destabilize the home, leading to unhealthy strife, sometimes even to raucous shouting matches that made life miserable for everyone. That's why God repeatedly demonstrated His rejection of this custom by consistently going outside this arrangement to fulfill His purpose. As with the birth of Isaac to Sarah, for example, so it was the same with the birth of Samuel to Hannah.

Though he could have flaunted his wealth and position, Elkanah was a generous and humble man who was devout in his Jewish faith and uncommonly kind in his relationships with others. Year after year, this man traveled to Shiloh to offer sacrifice to the Lord in obedience to Levitical law.

Shiloh was where the notorious duo of Hophni and Phinehas, the wicked sons of Eli, served as priests. These two men not only openly and unlawfully roasted their portion of the sacrifices, which, by coercion, were the best cuts of meat available, but they also strutted about the grounds with an air of superiority that made people cringe in disgust (I Sam. 2:12-17). What's more, they forced themselves sexually upon the women who served at the entrance to the Tabernacle, no doubt most of the time against their will. It was hard to worship under these conditions. Even Eli, their despairing father and the high priest, no longer had any control over them. Their very presence defiled the tabernacle.

As a measure of his dedication, however, Elkanah refused to use the situation as an excuse to stop worshipping there, even though he knew (indeed, all Israel knew) what was happening. When it was his turn to offer sacrifice, he would give portions of meat to each member of the family, but to Hannah, he would give a double portion "because he loved her" and because he knew that she was grieving over her barren condition (1 Sam. 1: 4-5).

While this was a comforting thing to do, it probably added insult to injury for Peninnah, who understood perfectly well what it meant. It no doubt added fuel to the fire of Peninnah's resentment and, therefore, to her desire for revenge. After all, in her mind, she was always on the short end of the stick when it came to Elkanah's heart.

There is no mention of him warning Peninnah to stop making Hannah feel even worse than she already did. This may have been because Peninnah was likely doing all of her taunting of Hannah behind his back. In contrast to the more aggressive Sarah, Hannah would have been far less likely to unload about it to Elkanah, who was already shouldering the burden of her depression. She was the kind of person who didn't want to weigh him down any further with her troubles than she had to.

When some people become depressed, they simply withdraw behind a veil of tears and become increasingly passive. That appears to have been the case with Hannah, as she was reduced to begging God in her prayers to intervene.

It's important to note that Elkanah never once blamed Hannah for her infertility. To the contrary, seeing Hannah's sad countenance, he persistently tried his best to cheer her up, even though he was honestly at a loss about what to say or do. Feeling he had to do something though, he clumsily tried to offer solace by asking her, "Don't I mean more to you than ten sons?" (vs. 8). He was attempting, of course, to remind her of his deep love for her, the renewed attention to which he hoped would help to alleviate her pain. More than likely, it only added, again unintentionally, to her guilt for being an inadequate wife.

That's the problem many men have with linear, purely logic-based thinking that suggests, if you do X, you should always get Y. That kind of thinking may be useful in business transactions, but it can backfire in the more emotionally nuanced environment of a despairing wife whose world has turned upside down. When all Hannah could think about was how empty and humiliated she felt, telling her that his love was worth more than having ten sons and giving her double portions of meat — as thoughtful as those things were — could never really have been expected to erase her pain.

When Elkanah found that nothing he tried made any difference, he must have felt indescribably helpless. Since men usually don't handle helplessness very well, he deserved great credit for not giving up on her, or worse, getting upset with her for failing to come out of her tailspin. Instead of telling her, out of his frustration, merely to "buck up", he continued to tenderly hang in there with her, which is what she most needed from him.

While at the Tabernacle, she stood and prayed earnestly for God's help, making a vow that if he would give her a son, she would give him back to serve the Lord for his entire life. Watching Hannah's lips continuing to move, but no voice being heard, Eli mistook her behavior for drunkenness, suggesting it wasn't the first time he thought he had detected intoxication in the Tabernacle. But once she told him what was really going on, and that she was making a vow to God, he stopped rebuking her and, instead, gave her a blessing.

After she finally conceived and bore a son, whom they named Samuel, Hannah told Elkanah about her vow and that she intended to go through with it after the child was weaned. The text doesn't record the emotional expression on his face when she told him, but we know he had patiently waited for a very long time for his primary wife to have a son who would then become his principal heir. Now his wife was telling him that she planned to take Samuel to Eli to minister in the tabernacle as she had promised God.

A wife could not just hand over her husband's son in compliance to some vow she had made without consulting her husband. The law made this quite clear:

> *"If a woman living with her husband makes a vow or obligates herself by a pledge under oath and her husband hears about it but says nothing to her and does not forbid her, then all her vows or the pledges by which she obligates herself will stand. But if her husband nullifies them when he hears about them, then none of the vows of pledges that came from her lips will stand. Her husband may confirm or nullify any vow she makes…These are the regulations the Lord gave Moses concerning relationships between a man and his wife…"* (Num. 30: 10-13, 16).

So, Elkanah had the legal right to cancel Hannah's vow. He even had the grounds to do that, given the men Samuel would have to serve under, such as Hophni and Phinehas. Even though it meant giving away his only son and heir by Hannah, he didn't flinch in letting her vow stand. He knew how much it meant to Hannah to acknowledge God's grace in erasing her (self-inflicted) shame for her barren condition. For the first time in years, her depression had lifted and she was happy once again. That's why he didn't hesitate to affirm her: *"Do what seems best to you. Stay here (home) until you have weaned him; only may the Lord make good his word"* (1Sam. 2: 23).

Proving the sincerity of his affirmation, when the time came, Elkanah even went with her to present the boy to Eli, the high priest, which no doubt made a world of difference to Hannah. In his love for her, he wanted for his wife to find peace and contentment. If that meant honoring her vow and giving his son away, then so be it, especially if it was a vow made to God. At the end of the day, he, too, saw Samuel's birth as a divine miracle. Indeed it was his vow as well. Besides, like Abraham, he trusted in the faithfulness of the Lord to supply him with other children for his posterity.

This was sacrificial love at its finest. He had displayed an unselfish level of compassion for his wife that would be forever imprinted on the intimacy of their marriage. Although his earlier attempts to comfort her had, at the time, seemed to fall on deaf ears, largely because of her state of utter despair, it's very likely that she warmly recalled them later. After all, she knew that it had come from his heart, as an honest expression of just how much he grieved over her unhappiness, even if he didn't know what to do about it.

Elkanah's tender empathy, his deep personal distress over his wife's wretched emotional condition, cannot be overestimated when considering the strength of their marriage. Every step Elkanah had taken to attend to Hannah's needs during her travail, though he was, at times, a bit clumsy at it, only deepened their bond with one another. Despite Peninnah's provocations, she had never been alone in her struggle and she knew it. He was always by her side, which is why she survived her ordeal with her marriage still emotionally intact.

There is simply no substitute for kindness and compassion to make it through difficult times and come out on the other end even stronger for the experience. We can thank Elkanah and Hannah for driving that point home in a special way.

They showed that you can't authentically follow our Lord for long without also becoming more like Him.

***

Points to Ponder

Every marriage undergoes ups and downs, times of struggle and times of triumph, times of worry and times of peace, times of pain and times of joy. As the writer of Ecclesiastes put it, there is a specific time for everything (Eccl. 3). These seasons of your life can come about by your own doing, but they also can be triggered by events completely outside your control. That's why it's a good idea to "divorce-proof" your marriage by deliberately cultivating those characteristics that have proven to be healing when you or those you love get roughed up by life.

One of those characteristics is the generous capacity to be kind and compassionate toward others. Kindness and compassion aren't just nice platitudes we utter until reality sets in and everything really hits the fan. Quite to the contrary. They are highly consequential attitudes, which, when translated into concrete behaviors, are critical to the success of any relationship. That's why, even without knowing exactly how to proceed, Elkanah nonetheless understood the importance of being sensitive to his wife's despair. He may not have fully comprehended the experience a woman went through when she couldn't bear children, but he could still see she was in need of a tender hand.

Even in his most vexing moments, Jesus always treated those He served exactly the same way. It was one of the reasons He was beloved by so many.

People who had been treated all their lives with ridicule and contempt by the Jewish leaders and their supporting cast of intellectuals, were startled to find a rabbi who was so accessible, bearing no sign of the prejudices of the upper classes. There was none of the insufferable hypocrisy they had grown accustomed to. Instead, His gentle and disarming presence, His love of justice, His compassion for the downtrodden endeared Him to all who came to listen to Him. Unlike the scribes and Pharisees, the credibility of Jesus' message was underscored by the authenticity of His character and the winsomeness of His person.

When Jesus spoke of the importance of forgiving one another for wrongs that had been committed against them and made it central to His teaching on prayer, they were able to grasp it, largely because they saw it played out in front of them. They beheld His compassion for Mary Magdalene, a woman no one wanted to get near; for the Samaritan woman at the well, who was shocked to find acceptance despite the fact that He knew all about her checkered past, and for the lepers, the castaways of society, on whom He physically placed His hands to the gasps of the crowd. Those are but a few of the examples of His revolutionary presence that told His listeners He was not your normal, run-of-the-mill, rabbi.

Think for a moment whether the kindness and compassion that Jesus brought to the table exists in your home on a daily basis. The harsh words said in frustration, the cold shoulder treatment which says your spouse isn't worth talking to, the eye rolls and sighs of contempt, the ridicule in opposing another point of view, or the intermittent accusations would all be re-appraised and discarded as beneath your marriage.

To those who would argue that they aren't Jesus, so we should stop expecting perfection, the only useful response is to tell them they're right, they're not Jesus. No one is asking them to be perfect. Such a charge is, in fact, a red herring.

Imperfection needn't stop anyone from aiming high in their marriage. Kindness and compassion can be deliberately cultivated. People are not born other-centered. To the contrary, we all start life self-centered, concerned exclusively about how things affect us. When we are young children, the world mostly revolves around us. Indeed, whole books have been written about the radical egocentrism of childhood.

As we get older, this hopefully changes in the process child psychologists call socialization. We know that not all homes are equal in producing these effects. So, early emotional conditioning and parentally-reinforced behaviors definitely play a major role in the final outcome. Nevertheless, it doesn't erase a person's ability to alter course. We are, after all, still capable of making decisions that deviate from our early training. Whether we let subsequent experience modify us and help turn us outward toward others, or whether we remain incubated in our tactless world of self-indulgence is ultimately a choice all of us must make. One thing is certain: If we refuse to make such changes, we'll no doubt become disillusioned about married life.

Marriage is a cooperative adventure which requires partners to pull the oars in the same direction. As Elkanah demonstrated, it involves a sacrificial commitment to the good of the other, a willing relinquishment of your will to God's in the fulfillment of His purpose for your relationship. As such, marriage is a covenant into which two people sacredly enter; it is dependent on the good will of each other, which, in turn, is conditioned on their mutual embrace of God's love and grace.

For the Christian, this covenantal arrangement involves the symbiosis of *two* intertwining covenants. The first is described by the Greek word, *suntheke*, which means an agreement among equals on condition of vows representing conditions mutually acceptable to both parties. This covenant, based on terms both agree on, is given its authority by the conditions on which it is made and assumes the veracity of each other's solemn word.

The second, which superintends the first, is described by the Greek word, *diatheke*, and is the unique biblical sense of covenant, meaning the entirety of the offer comes from God. It is the meaning that the Bible always uses for the concept of covenant, which involves participants who are decidedly *not* equal. Suffice it to say, it's impossible for God and man to meet on equal grounds. The holy and the profane can never really mix, at least not without profound sacrifice.

While *suntheke* refers to an ordinary covenant used in business transactions, social arrangements, and marriages among people on the same footing, *diatheke* refers not so much to an agreement as it does to *a will*. Man does not set the terms — you can't argue with God over the conditions of this covenant. Like a will, the terms of the biblical covenant, which is at the heart of our relationship with God, are not subject to negotiation. All the promises come from God. We are not responsible for any part of it. The only response that is asked of us is to accept or reject the terms of the covenant, much like we do any inheritance.

The first covenant, therefore, assures your mutual embrace of one another, accepting the responsibility to care for each other, and pledging fidelity to no other. The second covenant — the one that is the hope of your faith — gives this pledged union its fundamentally spiritual dimension and makes it a truly sacred journey under the cover of God's blessing. Together, they represent an indissoluble bond sealed by God and consecrated to His purpose. As Jesus Himself declared, "What God has joined together let not man put asunder" (Matt. 19: 6).

In the book of Judges, we read that God is repeatedly moved by compassion in response to His people's cries for help, even though they had fallen into sin and consequently had ended up being overrun by their enemies. As a result, He sent "judges" to rescue them from their oppressors.

The purpose of this book is to remind us that God brings His endless mercy and compassion to bear on each and every one of His children. Despite the fact that most of the problems we face are ones of our own creation, He doesn't deviate from His character. So, too, in the New Testament, we are encouraged to follow his example:

"Be imitators of God, therefore, as dearly beloved children and live a life of love, just as Christ loved us, and gave himself up for us as a fragrant offering and sacrifice to God" (Eph. 5: 1).

This is precisely what Elkanah was doing for his wife. Knowing that he was loved by God implanted in him the desire to love others like that. That's why he was doing his best to imitate God in sacrificing his own interests to serve his wife's needs. Was he perfect at it? No. But in the process his desire became hers as they shared that precious moment when Samuel was formally accepted for service in the tabernacle of the Lord.

That was the beginning of the profoundly significant ministry of the prophet Samuel, which spanned the transition from localized tribal authority practiced during the period of the Judges to the emergence of the united monarchy. Not only did Elkanah and Hannah witness the fruits of their decision to follow through on her vow, but God specifically blessed their marriage and enriched their family for doing so.

Elkanah's compassion had effects more far-reaching than anything he could ever have imagined. It not only cemented the bond he had with his wife, and with his Lord, but also changed the governing direction of Israel's history. Indeed, Samuel became the prophetic linchpin to the dawn of Israel's monarchy (1Sam. 9-10).

Part Six - Maturing Marriages

Chapter 13

David and Bathsheba: From Lust to Mature Love
2Samuel 11-12:25; 23

The story of David and Bathsheba is one of the most well-known stories in the Bible outside of the story of Jesus' birth in Bethlehem. It's a shameful story and quite possibly the lowest point in David's moral life, but it forever changed the course of his personal life. One might add that it changed the course of Israel's history, too.

One spring evening, David was having difficulty sleeping. He got up from his bed and walked on the roof of his palace. While there, he spotted a beautiful young woman bathing herself in a house nearby and was instantly captivated by her. He had not been on the prowl, but one glimpse of Bathsheba was enough to sexually arouse him. It's always good to keep in mind that lust can sometimes strike when you least expect it.

When he asked one of his assistants to find out about her, the man said, *"Isn't this Bathsheba, the daughter of Eliam, and the wife of Uriah, the Hittite?"* The rhetorical nature of his question indicated that he assumed David already knew her. His response was like, "Oh, you know who that is, David…. that's Bathsheba, you know, the daughter of Eliam, who's been around the palace since she was a kid."

David evidently didn't recognize her at a distance, possibly because he was close to fifty years of age and his eyesight may not have been what it used to be, unlike the vision of his young assistant. Since housing in Jerusalem was closely packed, an area for bathing on the rooftop would have likely been partitioned off for privacy. Neighbors were close enough to even converse with one another from their rooftops, where activities including sleeping were quite common, especially during the warm evenings of spring and summer.

Bathsheba would likely not have thought of privacy issues from above, which was where David's perch was, high up on the palace roof looming over the dense housing built just below it. Such homes grouped around the palace — call it "the palace district" if you like — were probably inhabited by the rich nobles of Jerusalem who especially valued their privacy.

The Bible explicitly notes that Bathsheba was ritually bathing "to purify herself from her uncleanness" (2 Sam. 11: 4), which meant that she had just completed her monthly menstruation cycle. It also meant that she was definitely not pregnant at the time. It can be safely concluded that she was not seductively bathing on her rooftop so that David could see her, but rather following the Mosaic Law in what she intended as a private cleansing.

At closer range, David would have recognized her as Bathsheba, since her father Eliam was one of his "thirty mighty men" (2 Sam.23: 24-39), whom he highly prized for his valor. That was also true of her heroic warrior husband Uriah the Hittite (vs. 39), who was most likely a converted Jew. What's more, she was the granddaughter of Ahithophel, David's chief personal counselor and advisor; this would have meant she was considerably younger than David. Ahithophel had been with David since the beginning of his reign and apparently Eliam had been with him from the time he was in the wilderness before he became king (2 Sam. 23: 34).

With all of her family connections to those who were frequent guests or participants in palace gatherings and honored activities, she likely grew up in David's shadow around the palace, watching him rule as God's anointed leader and listening to her father and grandfather talk about him in glowing terms. She was but a small child when David first became king. She no doubt heard him speak of the Lord many times, both in his public pronouncements and his private conversations in the palace.

She may very well have met and fallen in love with the illustrious Uriah when he had dropped by the palace to give reports on the front lines of the latest war. Eliam would not have hesitated to give the hand of his daughter in marriage to a man of such stature and accomplishment. Ahithophel would have looked upon their union with pleasure. The upshot of this is that together with her husband, they had all been frequent visitors at the palace over the years and knew each other very well.

So, David knew them intimately, which made his advances toward Bathsheba and his murder of Uriah all the more egregious. He had not only committed adultery and homicide, but he'd also abused his power as king, the position to which God appointed him. The problem started with David remaining in Jerusalem instead of being with his troops in the field of battle where he should have been (2 Sam. 11: 1). With too much idle time on his hands, he had increased his chances of using it unwisely. In this case, he allowed his baser instincts to be aroused in the fading light of an unusually quiet palace. In the course of time, he violated every principle of mindful living, foolishly thinking no one would notice, the typical palace scuttlebutt notwithstanding.

Curiously, there is no mention of Bathsheba's emotional or verbal response to David's seduction, except that she slept with him. Some argue that she was entirely an innocent victim; because it was an abuse of royal power, she felt there was little else she could do in the situation. Others contend that she went along with it because she was flattered by the king's interest in her and because she was momentarily aroused herself in that darkened bedroom. In other words, she was complicit in the affair.

We honestly cannot say beyond speculation and assumption what her state of mind was at the time. We just don't know. Given the urgency of the men sent to fetch her, it's entirely possible that she initially came to the palace under the impression that the king had some kind of news, perhaps bad news, to share either about her husband or her father, both of whom were engaged in battle at the time, or maybe about her grandfather who was getting along in years.

When she arrived, however, she no doubt quickly learned that there was a very different reason for her requested visit. How exactly David approached his liaison with her remains a mystery. Did he abruptly move into sexually seductive mode, or did he first talk about how lonely she might feel, living as she was without anyone to talk to or to connect with while her husband was away. Was he aggressive with her, as those who argue that it was rape believe, or was he gentle, wooing her softly into his bed, hoping she was attracted to him as well?

We will never know the answers to these questions, which is why it is a useless game to speculate as to what happened. The bottom line was that they had an illicit affair that resulted in an unanticipated pregnancy that threw them into a panic about what to do to cover it up. In David's desperation, after the failed attempt to surreptitiously get Uriah to have sex with his wife so the forthcoming pregnancy wouldn't be questioned, he did the unthinkable. He arranged to have Uriah killed in battle by having his men withdraw behind him, leaving him entirely exposed (2Sam.11:6-15). Uriah's death would be the excuse to bring Bathsheba into the palace as his wife.

In David's fevered mind, he might have imagined that his actions had noble overtones, suggesting that he was compassionate enough to rescue his chief warrior's wife from the travails of widowhood. But God knew the real score. Because God knew, so did His prophet Nathan. To tell the truth, there was probably a whisper campaign of gossip sweeping through the palace as well, given the suspicious timing of all these events. Still, the transition of Bathsheba had to be carried out swiftly after her seven days of mourning; otherwise, people outside the palace would know that not enough time had passed for the child to have been conceived after she became David's wife.

King David paid a steep price for all this subterfuge. He was disgraced by indulging his runaway lust, and worse, in his fear of being discovered for taking a faithful soldier's life in his ignominious attempt to cover up the resulting pregnancy. As a result, his life was never the same again. He deserved severe punishment, which he understood after being confronted by the prophet Nathan, who did not lay any blame at the feet of Bathsheba. When David plainly admitted, "I have sinned against the Lord" (2 Sam. 12: 13), he braced himself for the consequences.

After this incident, we see what seemed like a reversal in the control David had over the events of his life. He appeared to be more under the heel of events than he was in charge of them. The tragedies of Amnon's rape of his sister; Absalom's murder of his brother; his abortive attempt to seize the throne from his father; the betrayals of trusted advisors, and Joab's treachery with his army commander Amasa all came in relatively quick succession following David's ruinous indiscretion.

However, surprised by God's mercy, David didn't lose his throne or his life. He did lose four children, the first being the son born of his adulterous affair with Bathsheba, which was God's direct repudiation of what he had done. Over the course of David's reign, he also lost three more, each one experiencing a violent death. If any of you have lost a child, then you know the immense personal suffering David as a father must have gone through. For David, the pain was compounded by his awareness that these losses were, at least indirectly, the consequence of his own wrongdoing.

With Absalom's death he also lost his long-time, trusted counselor Ahithophel. At first, Ahithophel betrayed him by siding with his son in his attempt at a *coup d'état*, and later committed suicide after he saw that David had regained control. It's likely that Ahithophel had greatly resented David for destroying his granddaughter's life with her husband Uriah, who was his esteemed son-in-law. That may be why he had advised Absalom to deliberately have sex with ten of David's concubines as a demonstration of his power, so that "all Israel will hear that you have made yourself a stench in your father's nostrils" (2 Sam. 16: 21-22).

David finally understood how much wider the ripple effects of his sin were on those he had cared about. As difficult as it was, David learned by experience just how badly his sin had not only scarred the rest of his life but had also left others terribly wounded in his wake. The stain of it never really left him (2 Sam. 16: 5-12). Nor was it forgotten by the Gospel writer, Mathew, who referred to Bathsheba in his genealogy of Jesus as simply "the wife of Uriah".

Somewhere in all of this, David had come to deeply love Bathsheba. The special favor she enjoyed with him wasn't merely because he felt guilt for what he had done to her, though that must have had some effect on their marriage. Simply getting married is not a cure for the moral failures you've experienced in life. Rather it seems that when David got right with God, admitting his sin and accepting the consequences for his actions, he became more deeply connected to his Lord than ever before.

Though it's not described in the book of Samuel, given her pedigree, it's likely that Bathsheba also grieved over what had happened, regardless of whether she entered into the affair willingly or unwillingly. The Bible's silence about Bathsheba's motivations in all of these matters has been the subject of intense speculation. But if we follow the law of parsimony here, it may simply mean that the author's interest was primarily focused on David, since he was the king of Israel appointed by God and it was his royal house that was central to the history of his people.

Still, it's reasonable to assume that Bathsheba, like David, understood the implications of the loss of their child shortly after birth, since he was the progeny of illicit sex which she knew as well as anyone was displeasing to God. Sadly, Bathsheba's pain had become the collateral damage of David's calamitous decision to pursue a relationship with a married woman.

In comforting her, David wanted her to believe that they could start anew, this time with God's blessing. Now that she was his wife, he lay with her again in the hope that this new beginning could be marked with a new child, one who would grow up with the highest of their ideals as a man of God's own choosing. In giving to her what she had lost, David desperately wanted to make amends for everything he'd done to make Bathsheba feel dirty for being a party to such immoral behavior. He felt rightly responsible for everything that had happened.

By committing himself unreservedly to their marriage, and with his renewed commitment to following God's commandments, his love for Bathsheba grew accordingly. In time, like Uriah, he was apparently drawn to her, not merely for her beauty, but for the woman she was, a woman with the characteristic loyalty of her father Eliam and the wisdom of her counselor-grandfather Ahithophel. In any case, she seemed to stand out in the royal court and was the only wife at the end who was recorded as personally attending the death of her husband.

David would likely have agreed with that master craftsman with the pen, C.S. Lewis, who once remarked, *"When I have learnt to love God better than my earthly dearest, I shall love my earthly dearest better than I do now."* David's increasing love for God helped him to understand how God had blessed him with a wife who resolutely stood by his side when she could have easily resented him for what he'd done to her and made him feel small for his blatant hypocrisy.

Of all of his wives, Bathsheba seemed to exert more influence over David and his court than any of them. It was their son, Solomon, who was singled out as his successor to the throne. More important, while David lay on his deathbed initially unaware of Adonijah's attempt to subvert it, Bathsheba was there to see the commitment to his enthronement through. (1 Kings 1).

She also was loved and respected by Solomon. After he came to power, he was said to have provided her with a throne of her own; there she sat on his right hand as the queen mother, presumably serving as one of his advisors (1 Kings 2: 19). It was Solomon who asked God for the wisdom to rule righteously rather than making the selfish request for a long life or great wealth. It's tempting to think that this characteristic of discernment came from Bathsheba's judicious parenting. Indeed, it's notable that while King Solomon was guilty of making some wrong choices in his life, adultery was clearly not one of them.

While the marriage of David and Bathsheba had gotten off on the wrong foot, it not only became highly consequential for the Davidic line, but also key to the stability of David's rule, which placed the Lord at the center of national worship. Ironically it was his reprehensible decision to follow the path of his lust that spring evening that triggered a cascade of events that brought David to his knees in search of God's mercy.

What he learned was the power of God's forgiveness to transform his faith from mere lip service to internalized conviction to follow God's statutes. In the process, he learned how to really love a woman, not to use her as a prop, as he did with Michal, or not simply out of admiration for her mediation skills, as he did with Abigail, or even for other skills that could be useful to the crown. He learned to treat her as someone who was precious to him, whose thoughts and desires were important to him.

It's hard to say which was greater, David's transformation of Israel as a nation or Bathsheba's transformation of him as a husband. Either way, it represented monumental change.

***

Points to Ponder

Jesus raised not a few eyebrows when He expanded the definition of adultery to include one's lustful thought life:

> *"You have heard that it was said, 'Do not commit adultery'. But I tell you that anyone who looks at a woman lustfully has already committed adultery with her in his heart"* (Matt. 5: 27).

Jesus was simply explaining the spiritual reach that the Mosaic Law had on everyone who was listening to Him. Many Jews in that day had conveniently defined adultery as having relations with another man's wife. That left a wide range of virgins and prostitutes who didn't fall into the prohibited category. Jesus was making it clear that the sin of lust can even be birthed in the mind as well as in the body. He was underscoring their essential depravity, which was an affront to his public display of piety to the typical Pharisee.

At times lust is a difficult desire to control, but the mastery of it depends on the moral restraint that comes with diligently seeking God's desires. When it degrades a marriage or, in David's case, provides the basis for the marriage in the first place, the challenge is to turn that natural desire into an occasion for a renewal of your faith.

God has promised that He will honor that effort just as He forgave David who cried out to Him in repentance of his sin. Because he was finally ready for change without hesitation, God went to work on his heart.

For those who have not succumbed to this particular sin, there is always the danger of developing an attitude of moral superiority, which is merely sin by another name. The old cliché, "Those in glass houses shouldn't throw stones", was meant to expose the hypocrisy that sin so easily sets in motion.

As believers, it's incumbent upon us to pray earnestly for reconciliation rather than spend a single ounce of energy in condemnation. Besides, the traumatizing effect such betrayals inevitably have on relationships is itself a corrective that prompts change, at least to those whose hearts are not already hardened by habitual sin.

The marriage of David and Bathsheba demonstrates that relationships can survive such trauma, and even thrive, providing the partners are committed to the marriage and are dependent on God's healing touch. Often, however, when marriage is preceded by a moral lapse, one or the other partner carries a burden of guilt into the relationship that can have a profound effect on their wholeness as a couple, including their sexual life together. It's critically important that this emotional undercurrent be addressed early, preferably during pre-marriage counseling, before it turns into a tidal wave of pain and miscommunication.

It's important to note that David did not let his own guilt and sorrow keep him from paying attention to the urgent needs of Bathsheba. She needed to forgive herself of the death of her newborn and to deal with the circumstances of Uriah's untimely death. She needed to hear that David was remorseful for what he'd done. She needed to have hope for the future that things would get better. Above all, she needed to be loved and reassured that David wouldn't abandon her after their deceased child was no longer a reason to be together.

By all accounts, David did step up to the plate. Unfortunately, many don't. But David proved to be an honorable husband with her, making Bathsheba the center of his affections and favor. It no doubt took a long time for the necessary healing to be completed, but they both were in it for the long run.

When David learned that the lives of Bathsheba and Solomon were endangered by Adonijah's clandestine attempt to unjustly wrest the crown for himself, he immediately swung into action, even though he was in his dying days. Yes, such action was necessary to make certain that his choice of Solomon as his successor was honored, but it's likely what most galvanized him into action was the fact that he knew Adonijah would otherwise murder his beloved wife and son. The very thought of that tore his heart in two.

It was his final heroic rescue, but it was the most important one.

This is the inspiration we can draw from the marital life of King David: That a man can act so egregiously with a woman, yet with God at his side, change so dramatically that in his last act as king he would order his personal guard to save her life and that of their son is testimony to what God can do to the heart of a man. He began his marriage with Bathsheba in a climate of humiliation but ended it in a climate of love and devotion.

Is not this the whole point of redemption?

Chapter 14

Hezekiah and Hephzibah: Solace for Parental Disillusionment
2Kings 18-20: 2Chronicles 29-32

Hezekiah, the twelfth king of Judea and son of the wicked King Ahaz, was a man of remarkable inspiration, a godly man living among an ungodly people who had sunk to their lowest moral and spiritual level in their nearly 300 year history. He inherited a nation that was a shrunken remnant of its glory days under King Uzziah, a nation which had become a weakened vassal to the powerful and sprawling Assyrian Empire. It had also become a sewer of depravity.

Only a few years earlier, in 722 BC, Judah had witnessed the utter destruction of its sister state of Israel by these same Assyrians. Israel had been an unrepentant nation of Jews that had become so steeped in idolatry that God had turned his back on her, bringing the catastrophic consequences of its desolation. Vast numbers of Israelites from that nation had been carted off to Assyria in bondage, never to be heard from again. A similar fate awaited Judah if they didn't straighten out their act and recover the purity of their historic faith.

Enter King Hezekiah, who, after the death of his father, began his own reign in 716 BC. Immediately, he started removing the high places where idol worship took place; he destroyed the sacred stones used in that worship and cut down the Asherah poles. He even broke into pieces the bronze snake Moses had used centuries earlier (Num. 21:4-9), which the people had pulled out of storage and had begun to burn incense to it as an icon of worship. It seemed as if the people were willing to worship almost anything that wasn't nailed down.

He also restored the instruction in the Torah, the daily services in the Temple, and the pilgrimages of devout Jews to Jerusalem. Once again, he wanted to normalize the worship of the Lord as part of the architecture of Jewish culture. He rightly saw it as the only real pathway to the survival of his people.

We are told that the iconoclastic King Hezekiah was unique among the royals of Judah's history: *"He trusted in the Lord, God of Israel. There was no one like him among all the kings of Judah, either before him or after him; he held fast to the Lord and did not cease to follow him"* (2 Kings 18: 5-6). He was keenly aware of the disaster his father had been as king, corrupting Judah with an endless parade of idolatries and weakening it by toadying up to the Assyrians, meanwhile losing wars on almost every front. As a result, Hezekiah was determined to overturn nearly every foreign and domestic policy his father ever pursued.

He was enormously successful at it, too. Besides all of his much needed religious reforms, he refused to serve the king of Assyria, defeated the Philistines as far as Gaza, and neutralized his other neighbors who had opposed Judah in the past. Perhaps the pivotal moment of his reign came several years later when King Sennacherib of Assyria laid siege on Jerusalem, intending to completely destroy it (701 BC).

A massive Assyrian army had swept through and captured the cities and towns in much of the surrounding Judean countryside and had now assembled and encamped just outside Jerusalem. Sennacherib sent messengers telling Hezekiah that he had his capital city surrounded and was poised to take it with ease, so that his best course of action was to surrender and save his people from unnecessary bloodshed. In delivering their message with insufferable arrogance, Sennacherib's men taunted the Judean soldiers on the city wall, telling them they didn't stand a chance. They mocked their religion and blasphemed their God by claiming He was not strong enough to defeat them.

Hezekiah instantly turned to the prophet Isaiah for guidance on what to do under these foreboding conditions. Isaiah reassured the king that God was well-aware of their blasphemy and would not only defeat them but prophesied that their king would be cut down by the sword when he returned to his own country. Despite further threats and taunts from Sennacherib, the emboldened Hezekiah went up to the Temple and defiantly prayed for Judah's deliverance:

> *"It is true, O Lord, that the Assyrian kings have laid waste these nations and their lands. They have thrown their gods into the fire and destroyed them, for they were not gods, but only wood and stone, fashioned by men's hands. Now, O Lord our God, deliver us from his hand, so that all kingdoms on earth may know that you alone, O Lord, are God"* (2 Kings 19: 17-19).

That same night the angel of the Lord struck down one hundred and eighty-five thousand men in the Assyrian camp. When Sennacherib awoke the next morning, he looked with horror over a field strewn with nothing but dead bodies. So he broke camp and withdrew back to Ninevah in humiliating defeat. Later he was assassinated by his sons while he was praying in the temple of his god, confirming Isaiah's prophecy.

The news of this victory spread quickly among the nations of the world, all of whom were astonished that tiny Judah could defeat Sennacherib's siege of Jerusalem. In short order, Hezekiah became quite famous, with the king of Babylon sending emissaries to congratulate him, as well as to wish him a speedy recovery from a severe illness that nearly took his life shortly after his deliverance from the Assyrian army. God, however, mercifully granted him fifteen more years to live in response to his desperate plea for more time.

Others, encouraged as they were by Judah's defiance, secretly hoped to garner his support for their increasing resistance against the Assyrian Empire. It began a movement that continued to gather steam over the next century until it led finally to the defeat of the Assyrian Empire by the insurgent Babylonians.

During all of these events, Hezekiah was faithfully served by his wife Hephzibah, a godly companion whose name was itself a statement of her righteous conduct. The names given to individuals in the Old Testament frequently predicted or foreshadowed either the nature of their character or the roles they would play in the history of God's people.

In the original Hebrew, Hephzibah means, "My (God's) delight is in her" and is found in only two places in the Old Testament, 2 Kings 21:1 and Isaiah 62:4. While Hephzibah is identified as the wife of Hezekiah and mother of Manasseh in the first passage, in the Isaiah reference, the term is strikingly used to signal a transformation, a new beginning in Israel's restoration to a place of God's favor. It paints a beautiful picture of Israel's change from a deserted and desolate people to the hope of their renewed faith in God's protective embrace.

When a term in the Bible is used sparingly it can suggest that its meaning carries the power of a unique or exceptional quality. Hephzibah is an exquisitely descriptive term that conveys the idea of God cherishing His fellowship with the subject of His affection. Because the ancient Israelites understood the significance of a name as pertaining to character, or even to prophecy, they would have likely interpreted the name of Hezekiah's wife as indicative of God's favor toward her. They would have understood further the qualities she had that merited her name, qualities which would perfectly describe her as a woman who was obedient to God's commandments.

The convictions of a wife like Hephzibah would have served to lift up the spirit of hope and optimism in God's power, much like Isaiah did with his message of hope to the distressed nation of Israel. What a gift she must have been to Hezekiah, especially in those dark days of the Assyrian siege or in the difficult years of turning an obstinate people back to their Abrahamic heritage.

When he prayed fervently in the Temple for God's deliverance from the hand of Sennacherib, no doubt Hephzibah was in her palace quarters on her knees pleading for God's grace on behalf of her husband. They were a couple who took seriously the task of serving God and His people.

Ancient Jewish tradition, which finds its source in the Babylonian Talmud, claims that Hephzibah was the daughter of the prophet Isaiah. If that were the case, he would have been comparing his own feelings of joy over his daughter to the joy God will feel over the restoration of His people. Whether or not it's true that she was his daughter, she was certainly known to the prophet, since he served as the voice of God during her husband's reign. At the very least, Isaiah's familiarity with her may have influenced his injection of her name into his prophecy about the future redemption of Israel.

While they successfully nurtured a godly marriage, it was entirely another matter when it came to their son. Hephzibah had the distinction of being the wife of the most righteous king to ever rule over the nation of Judah. At the same time, she was the mother of Manasseh, perhaps the most wicked king to ever sit on the throne. It was a heartache she had to bear alone in the later years of her life because of the death of her beloved Hezekiah. As the queen mother, she must have grieved every day she was alive during her son's rule, as she was forced to witness his dismantling of virtually every reform her husband had enacted.

There is no mention in the biblical record when Manasseh's heart began to harden to the truths of the Torah. He was born after Hezekiah's serious illness in 709 BC, six years after his evil grandfather Ahaz had died. So he never knew his grandfather personally, though he had undoubtedly heard all the stories of his terrible reign.

He became a co-regent with his father at the age of twelve, presumably because after his brush with death Hezekiah feared he wouldn't otherwise have the chance to train his son in royal administrative duties before it was too late. Hezekiah always diligently attended to the details of governance. Manasseh served in his co-regent capacity until his father's death in 686 BC, when he became the sole monarch over Judah.

There is no evidence that he tried to subvert his father's rule during his co-regency by openly violating the religious reforms Hezekiah had put into place. There would have been a major fissure between them if he had tried. In general, as a teenage co-regent, Manasseh gave the appearance of a son who agreed with his father's policies and that he would carry forward all the reforms that his father had made.

That appearance vanished into thin air the moment his father died. Much to his mother's chagrin, the hidden idolater in him came out of the closet and became the real force behind the Manasseh administration. Perhaps Hezekiah and Hephzibah saw some troubling signs in him, maybe a rebellious streak of some sort, which they tried to address by giving him more responsibilities. Possibly he was just adept at keeping his true sentiments entirely to himself so that his parents were unaware what was brewing underneath. Either way, they were unable to stop him from assuming complete control once his father died.

At some point, Hephzibah must have wondered what went wrong during Manasseh's growing up years that would have so twisted his thinking into becoming the corrupt autocrat that he became. Was he influenced by sons of pagan courtiers with whom he hung around as a boy? Did he have a teacher in the royal household who corrupted his mind with blasphemous ideas? Did he spend too much time reading the court records of his grandfather's reign, perhaps idealizing his rule in the absence of any experience with him? Did she and Hezekiah pay too little attention to his idiosyncrasies that may have foretold of problems down the road?

She was most likely at a loss to explain why he went off the rails with his spiritual life, not to mention his failure to act prudently as a head of state. She may have felt somehow guilty for how he turned out. To be sure, she must have spent more than a few hours on her knees, praying that he would turn from his evil ways and embrace the God he ostensibly worshipped in his youth.

In her years as queen mother, her heart must have been breaking over what she saw and heard her son doing. After all, Judah had become a surreal world of runaway idolatry of the worst kind, of foreign policy decisions that defied even common sense, and of an intolerant king who brooked no dissent.

It was said that under Manasseh's leadership, Jerusalem was filled from end to end with the shedding of innocent blood. Hephzibah was living in a nightmare of ever increasing blasphemy, and exploding violence in the streets, fearfully and helplessly watching her people being catapulted toward the brink of national suicide.

What had started out for Hephzibah as a marvelous journey of religious revival with her husband King Hezekiah had now ended in the horrors of her son's maniacal rule that destroyed everything Hezekiah had done to redeem the nation. She no doubt retained a mother's love for Manasseh, which made all that transpired after he became king that much more painful. Worse yet, she no longer had her husband there to console her in the midst of her despair.

She probably replayed scenes from his childhood over and over in her mind, wondering where evil began to get a grip on his heart. Such rumination accomplishes little, other than keeping a person in a perpetual prison of guilt and turmoil. They do it anyway because they become almost obsessive in their desire to know where things went wrong. At length, she was called upon to mature further in the peace of the Spirit in ways she never anticipated.

Despite the fact that she was the queen mother, she apparently had no say in any of her son's decisions. She could only look on with dread, wondering when the next shoe of blasphemy was going to drop. We don't know exactly when she died, but it's likely that it was long before Manasseh was hauled off in chains to Babylon as the result of a foolish and unnecessary war.

So, she didn't live to see the remarkable transformation of Manasseh, who while sitting in a dark, dank prison cell in Babylon finally called out to God for forgiveness, promising to make things right if he ever regained his freedom. In his mercy, God honored Manasseh's newfound humility and restored him to his throne. From that point on, he was a different man, doing his best to reverse all that he had done to destroy the worship of the Lord, God of Israel.

Hephzibah died a broken-hearted mother, probably still wondering where she went wrong, but she never stopped loving God, joining the faithful remnant of Judah who remained steadfast in their worship despite the unruly environment in which they lived.

Though she may have had difficulty accepting it, she was not responsible for her son's rebellion against the Lord. As godly parents, Hezekiah and Hephzibah had raised Manasseh to be a God-fearing young man. To that end, she had to settle for knowing she had done her best and to trust the Lord that He would work in her son's life.

It was *her son's* decision to walk away from everything he'd been taught, but his day of reckoning finally came by way of an Assyrian invasion that landed him in a Babylonian jail. Once again, God was faithful in answering Hephzibah's prayers and forgave him, unleashing in Manasseh a spiritual reformation that doubtlessly shocked even the most cynical courtiers.

Redemption, at long last, had come to the throne.

***

Points to Ponder

Often the first months and years go relatively smoothly in a marriage where the hindrances are few and the household responsibilities are light. Marital partners are, for the most part, free to do what they want together. They have more discretionary funds available for spending on entertainment and other desires and have friends readily accessible with whom they can continue to socialize.

All of this changes when children come into the picture. Suddenly, they are not as free as they once were, often having to limit get-togethers with their friends to attend their children. They must redirect funds to child care, clothing, feeding, and visits to the pediatrician, which also places a limit on the affordability of their previous lifestyle. In other words, life changes considerably, changes which present unexpected challenges to adapt and adjust to the new responsibilities of a family.

As a result, a new set of conflicts may arise around the issue of parenting styles, including the credibility gap that can exist between permissive and stricter philosophies of discipline. Not infrequently, one marital partner purposely relaxes the rules while the other, who is trying to compensate for the lack of discipline, tries to legalistically run a tight ship. This inevitably means arguments with each other over disciplinary approaches and their effects on the behavior problems of their children.

Divorces have been known to occur over these kinds of conflicts, especially when one or the other spouse interprets their differences as evidence of being unloved or disrespected. They often wonder how they became so easily alienated from one another. They didn't anticipate the fact that raising children can be a challenging business and never knew they would clash so vehemently over such issues. This is often the case when they have neglected to meaningfully discuss these things before they had children.

But there is another unanticipated outcome that also can drive a wedge between spouses, at least among those whose faith is central to their lives. One of the most gut-wrenching experiences for Christian parents to go through is to watch their son or daughter abandon their faith and head in a direction that is completely foreign to everything they had hoped for them. Such was the disheartening experience of Hephzibah with her son Manasseh in ancient Judah.

This happens with far greater frequency than most people imagine. It sometimes can even lead to a strain in the marriage, with each partner harboring silent (or not so silent) accusations against the other for perceived failures in parenting. The truth is, we all make mistakes as parents; there is no one who does everything right, even if they think they do. To believe that wayward offspring only come from either dysfunctional homes where poor or inadequate parenting is the norm, or from homes divided over disciplinary tactics, is to adhere to a myth.

Many young people who come from loving Christian homes, even ones where the parents were on the same page in terms of discipline, nevertheless begin to question their faith at some point. Some of them become easy prey for an atheistic or agnostic professor they admire, especially one who takes perverse pleasure in dismantling a student's faith. For others, it may be an acquired friend who is into alternative, sometimes exotic, belief systems they've never before encountered. Or they may simply have been exposed to adverse social media influences, like pornography or other sexually explicit sites (which are openly accessible, even in public libraries), that have altered their view of themselves and others, often adding underlying guilt and unrelenting secrecy to the mix.

These are but a few of the possible factors in driving young people into the arms of self-defeating thoughts and behavior. Young adults are responsible for their own choices in life, regardless of the kind of home they come from. It's easy to forget that fact when you pillory yourself (or your spouse) instead for the wayward tendencies of your children.

If God, our heavenly Father, did what self-flagellating parents do, He would have been lamenting over His own inadequacies when His people, the children of Israel, abandoned their worship of Him in favor of a corrupt idolatry. Rather than encountering a depressed, self-debasing God, we find Him assured in His holiness and righteousness pronouncing judgment on His people who have rebelled against His commandments. No one in their right mind would find a God who blamed our sin on His failure as a Father worthy of worship. He would more likely elicit our pity.

You may argue that you're not God, so you don't have His omniscience or power. True, but notice He doesn't use His power to coerce His children to follow Him. That's because He created them with free will. Love, of which He is the embodiment, does not exist in a vacuum. It needs freedom to flourish and grow.

Likewise, we need to see our children that way. We equip them the best way we can, mistakes and all, and then give them the freedom to make their own decisions, good or bad. Your job as a parent is to work your way out of a job and hand over the responsibility of living to your children when they reach adulthood. It is not to "force" them to do what is right. Not even God does that.

Some cling to the proverb that states, "Train up a child in the way he should go and when he is old he will not turn from it" (Proverbs 22: 6), believing that it's somehow a guarantee that children rightly raised by godly parents will remain steadfast in the faith as adults. If that were true, then the element of free choice would be a mirage and, therefore, so also would be God's love in creating us with a free will.

Besides, it would be a basic misunderstanding of the purpose of proverbs, which is to lay down principles that are *generally true* as applied to a specific situation; as with all generalities, proverbs are not without exceptions. It's those exceptions that reveal the workings of free will, the wild card in any prediction about how things will turn out. Still, countless Christian couples who've seen their children abandon the faith have unnecessarily endured paroxysms of false guilt because of a passage they've grossly misinterpreted.

The Hebrew word used for training up a child actually refers to both his domestic and moral education, preparing him for the future. It generally means skill-building based on a child's personality and temperament, as well as on his natural talents and abilities, all within the God-fearing framework of faithful piety.

Part of this maturation process is taking responsibility for your own decisions and behavior. The Apostle Paul points this out when he describes the difference between a child and an adult:

"When I was a child, I talked like a child, I thought like a child, I reasoned like a child. When I became a man, I put childish ways behind me" (1 Cor. 13: 11).

Part of childish thinking is not taking responsibility for yourself, but expecting others (parents, in particular) will pick up the slack. It's not the parent's job to carry that responsibility forever without delegating it to the adult child. Indeed, *that* would be parental malpractice!

You may agonize over the decisions they make, but the moment you automatically blame yourself for those decisions is the same moment you withdraw the responsibility you gave them for their behavior in the first place. Some parents feel desperate enough that they feel compelled to unwisely intervene, usually out of misguided combination of love and guilt. While it may be extremely difficult to watch your adult children take a spiritual path contrary to your own, arguing theology with them is usually not a good idea.

On the other hand, it can be useful to ask them thoughtful questions designed to respectfully get them to think through their positions. It's important for them to know what they're for, not just what they're against, and to be able to hear themselves say it out loud. You may not like the answers you get. That's where it's crucial not to get angry with them (which may understandably come from your frustration), but rather to treat their thinking with patience and respect.

In the long run, however, it's your adult children who must take full responsibility for the lifestyle they embrace, just as you did before them when you became an adult. That's simply part of growing up. The prophet Ezekiel explained it this way when he was speaking about determining culpability for sin:

> *"The child will not share the guilt of the parent, nor the parent share the guilt of the child. The righteousness of the righteous will be credited to them, and the wickedness of the wicked will be charged against them"* (Ezekiel 18: 20).

He was reaffirming the Law as stated in Deuteronomy 24: 16. So, if God makes that distinction in determining culpability, then so should we. It's worth repeating for those needlessly suffering from self-imposed guilt over their children's apostasy that the Bible makes it clear no guarantee comes with parenting. Certainly, Manasseh was the poster child for that reality.

What it does teach is that throughout life every parent should continue to quietly model the virtues they want their children to have. Living what you've taught your children never becomes obsolete, nor is it necessarily a lost cause to hope that they will return to the faith. The grieving father in Jesus' parable of the prodigal son was an unambiguous example of this truth.

If your children can't see Christ in how you respond when you encounter the unexpected setback, then all the words of wisdom you have to impart to them will not amount to much. It's useful to remember that actions do speak louder than words.

That became Hephzibah's challenge with Manasseh. If you have lost a child to the world's enticements, it's your challenge, too.

Chapter 15

King Xerxes and Esther: The Influence of a Godly Wife

The Book of Esther, Chaps. 1-10

Most scholars believe that the king identified in the Hebrew text of Scripture as Ahasuerus, who ruled at the time of Esther, was one and the same as King Xerxes I, which is a transliteration of the Greek form of the Persian name Khshayarshan. He was the son of Darius I, the fourth emperor of the Achaemenid (Persian) Empire, and his reign covered a span of 20 years (485-465 BC). Xerxes had a winter palace in the capitol city of Susa in the lower Zagros Mountains about 160 miles east of the Tigris River in present day Iran. This is where the events recorded in the book of Esther took place.

Up to that time, the vast Persian Empire was the largest ever known and included over 127 provinces stretching from India to the east to Cush on the continent of Africa to their west. So when he held meetings for official business or banquets for celebration, when all the military leaders, princes, and nobles of the provinces were expected to attend, they were enormous gatherings.

Xerxes had a mercurial temperament and was given to suddenly triggered rage where everyone around him cowered in fear; he displayed equally contagious periods of exuberance and festivity, during which he was known to hold lavish banquets. He was a man of intense tastes, renowned for his heavy drinking and his powerful sexual appetite. Yet he was also a generous man who had a reputation for richly rewarding those loyal to the throne. Certainly, marriage to a man like this had its rigorous challenges, which Queen Vashti, Esther's predecessor, unfortunately discovered.

By no means a modest man, Xerxes liked to parade his wealth and the splendor and glory of his majesty. On the occasion of one of his banquets, during which he had been drinking heavily, he demanded that his wife be brought to the huge dining hall to put her beauty on display before the crowd of notable men of the realm. He wanted them all to admire his taste in women.

Queen Vashti refused to come. Perhaps she hated the exploitive character of his demand. On the other hand, as some have suggested, it might have been because she wasn't feeling up to it, since she was possibly pregnant at the time with a son who would eventually become the king's successor to the throne. In any case, Xerxes was furious with her and humiliated that she defied his order and exerted her independence before the court. Consequently, he had her stripped of her title as queen and banished from the palace. This did not necessarily mean exile, especially if she was pregnant, but rather could have meant that she was sent to the royal harem to assume lifelong anonymity. Such a consequence would have been far more humiliating, given her prior exalted status as queen.

Upon advice of his counsel, he was determined to show that the women of the realm had better not follow the example of Vashti and despise their husbands; otherwise the empire would be filled with disrespect and marital discord. This meant they would not tolerate women having more of a voice than men in their marriages. Strike another victory for male dominance!

Four years passed before another virgin, a young Jewess named Esther, was selected to take Vashti's place as queen. Though it appeared that Xerxes was largely led along by his advisors, the narrative shows that this was another instance of God orchestrating events to protect His people.

Esther, whose Hebrew name was Hadassah, had been the ward of her first cousin Mordecai (the Babylonian name given him), who was a Jew of the tribe of Benjamin, as was she. Mordecai was believed to have been a descendent of Kish, his great-grandfather who was deported to Babylon along with Judah's young King Jehoiachin, and other members of the royal family and the Jewish intelligentsia in 597 BC. While living in Babylon,

Mordecai adopted the daughter of his uncle Abihail after he and his wife both died and left Esther an orphan.

After the Babylonians were defeated by Cyrus the Great and the Persians, and the Jews were freed from captivity, he and Esther migrated to Susa. There, he became an administrative officer in the court, which is why the Bible tells us that he was usually found at the king's gate. He had warned Esther not to tell anyone about their Jewish background, apparently because he feared there might be some anti-Semitic types among the population of Susa, or at least among the courtiers who worked for the king.

Esther was described as a particularly beautiful virgin, which made her a prime candidate to "audition" to become one of the king's concubines, if not the queen. She expressed no interest in becoming either, but she was taken by the king's men to the palace, meaning she was conscripted for such candidacy without any real say in the matter. She (along with the others) spent the next year being given a variety of luxurious beauty treatments to make them extremely alluring for their visit with the king.

Common among monarchs the world over, physical beauty was a priority with the pampered and lustful Xerxes. Out of all who were brought before the king (and who were expected to sleep with him overnight), Esther was clearly his most preferred, which is why she was chosen to become the next queen. The others, after they had spent their night with the king, never saw him again unless he happened to call for one of them. It was duty, not love, which usually served as the basis for marriage to a king of the ancient Near East. Despite the fact that Xerxes was a polygamist, Esther proved that a wife can exert considerable influence on her royal husband, especially if he becomes rather smitten by her.

The boastful Xerxes, with his penchant for exhibitionism, was not without his enemies, both outside and inside his kingdom, where there lurked men in high places who either hated him or wanted his power and access to his wealth. In fact, he was eventually assassinated by the head of his bodyguard detail.

During Esther's reign as queen, Mordecai happened to overhear a plot being hatched to kill Xerxes. He immediately reported the matter to Esther, who informed the king, explicitly giving Mordecai the credit for being her source. Because of her early warning, the king had the men promptly arrested and executed. This demonstration of loyalty tightened his bond with Esther even further. Although Mordecai was the one who actually saved the life of the king, he was not initially recognized for his heroism.

Later, when Haman, one of the king's chief advisors, was promoted and given a seat of honor greater than all the other nobles (much like a prime minister), Mordecai refused to bow down to him as did all of the other officials of the court. Though he had no difficulty bowing before the king, he was not about to lower himself before an arrogant, swaggering courtier like Haman. Mordecai had apparently confided in his fellow officials at the king's gate that he was a Jew, implying that he was taught only to bow in honor to God and the head of state, not to anyone of less authority, especially one who was undeserving as Haman.

Haman was outraged and, having learned who Mordecai's people were, immediately began to plot his revenge by killing not only Mordecai but also the entire population of Jews throughout the whole kingdom. This would have included Jews who were living in Palestine and worshipping in the newly rebuilt Temple. In other words, Haman's plan was to wipe out every Jew in the Persian Empire in an anti-Semitic pogrom, the likes of which the world had never seen before. As genocidal as it was, he was preparing to become the Adolf Hitler of the 5th Century BC.

Haman was identified as an Agagite, which some scholars argue meant that he was a descendent of Agag, king of the Amalekites (1 Sam. 15: 8). The Amalekites had been among the most hardened enemies of Israel, beginning shortly after their exodus from Egypt. While those armed conflicts occurred centuries earlier, it's very possible that an anti-Semitic prejudice had lingered on, having been transmitted from generation to generation of Amalekite descendants. It would explain why Haman was so eager to destroy an entire people simply because one man had responded to him in a way he didn't like.

In presenting his evil plan to exterminate the "enemies of the state" for Xerxes' authorization, Haman did not reveal they were all of one nationality, the Jews. The king merely believed they were a rabble of agitators arrayed against his rule and the laws of the land. He gave his consent, but to speed things along, Haman had the gallows built for Mordecai's execution, which he planned to carry out even before he sent out the order to all the provinces to kill all the Jews in a single day. That date was chosen by lot (called a *pur*). As it turned out, the date gave the Jewish people almost a year to mentally prepare for their slaughter.

The next night, being unable to sleep, the king called in one of his servants to read to him out of the book of the chronicles, which was the record of his reign. By God's invisible hand, the servant turned to the page that described Mordecai's heroism in saving the king's life from the plot to assassinate him. Realizing Mordecai had never been rewarded for his great deed, he directed Haman to honor him in the manner that Haman (thinking he was the one to be acclaimed) had suggested.

After Mordecai was formally hailed as a hero, he returned to the king's gate where he wept bitterly, since he was already aware of the plot to eradicate the Jewish people. He realized his actions had put all of his people in jeopardy. As soon as he got wind of the plan, he raced to the palace and sent word to Esther of what was happening; he pleaded with her to intercede with the king on behalf of her people to stop the madness.

After some hesitation, knowing the king could have her put to death for daring to go to him without first being summoned by him, she agreed to do it. "If I perish, I perish," were her exact words in response to Mordecai's observation that she would die anyway if Haman had his way. Mordecai added that Esther may have come to her royal position exactly for a time such as this. He could do no more than to warn Esther to put an end to Haman's genocidal plan.

To Esther's relief, King Xerxes was delighted to see her and extended to her his golden scepter, welcoming her to approach the throne. His favor of her was never more critical than at this moment. She invited his majesty to a private banquet she had planned and asked him to bring along Haman as his guest, which he heartily agreed to do. After all, he was going to have his two favorite people sit down with him for a sumptuous meal together. What could be better than that? Besides, Xerxes was promised to finally get the answer to his question as to what particular request she wanted to make of him.

At the conclusion of not one but two banquets on consecutive days, which Esther gave in honor of the king and his chief advisor, she finally made her appeal to the king, as Haman sat nearby, listening intently. *"If I have found favor with you, O king, and, if it pleases your majesty, grant me my life—this is my petition. And spare my people. For I and my people have been sold for destruction and slaughter, and annihilation"* (Esther 7:3-4).

In the process, she went on to reveal her own Jewish ethnicity. Aghast at her request, the king asked who in the world would do such a terrible thing as wiping out the entire Jewish race. That's when she pointed directly to Haman and exclaimed, "The adversary and enemy is this vile Haman."

For Haman, the jig was up. The king, in his rage, immediately ordered Haman to be seized and he was executed that day on the gallows he'd erected for Mordecai. To counter the order Haman had sent out to the citizens of Persia to kill every Jew in their province, another decree was issued on the king's behalf that granted the Jews in every city in the realm the right to protect themselves. Mordecai was elevated to take Haman's post to make sure that the new order was carried out.

The Jews were now empowered to destroy any armed citizen groups that might attack them. As a result, over seventy-five thousand of their anti-Semitic enemies were killed on the same day that Haman's order had designated for the Jews' slaughter.

While it's a dramatic story of God's intervention on behalf of his people through Esther and Mordecai, it is also an example of the powerful influence a woman can have in her marriage. Esther was clearly a woman of destiny, whose marriage was the crucial conduit through which the king first became aware of the plight of her people, and then, ordered Haman's death, overturning the edict issued for annihilation of the Jews.

Digging deeper into their marriage, it's interesting to note that, while it was initially a typically arranged union between a king and his consort, King Xerxes developed a true affection and respect for Esther. This was not merely because she was young and beautiful (which was, no doubt, the initial attraction), but also because she was intelligent, deferential, gracious, and humble. She made him a better man because her behavior brought out the best in him.

Though he was rough around the edges, too showy, and too prone to drink to excess, he had a decent sense of justice and did not share Haman's anti-Semitic bias. In fact, he (as well as his predecessor, Cyrus the Great) was generally very supportive of pluralistic policies that acknowledged the right of peoples of different nationalities to live and worship according to their own customs, provided they obeyed Persian law.

King Xerxes was the world's most powerful monarch — his word was absolute — yet he was appalled at the thought that anyone, least of all someone in his own government, would even think about the genocide of an entire people. Whatever flaws he had, unjustly hating a people merely because of their ethnicity was not one of them.

That's something Esther came to deeply respect and honor in her husband. In spite of his many faults, she discovered the attributes of Xerxes that she could truly admire, which made her life as queen far more satisfying, even pleasing at times. It undoubtedly strengthened their bond of trust with one another.

She had learned the invaluable lesson in marriage that it's always best to look for the traits in your mate that you can fully appreciate rather than merely focusing on the traits you don't like, which only increases your agitation and dissatisfaction. Many a marriage has survived difficult times precisely because of this principle. In this case, Esther was banking on her husband's belief in pluralism and fair play.

Perhaps Esther's greatest asset was found in her ability to properly prepare her husband for grievous news. In first honoring him with a banquet, she was implicitly telling him that his integrity and judgment as a leader were highly esteemed and deserved her recognition. She was purposely appealing to his best instincts, which she needed to come to the fore in order for him to realize the heinous nature of Haman's plans.

Her strategy worked; after six years of marriage to Xerxes, she had gotten to know his sense of basic decency. She could definitely relate to a man without a trace of racial prejudice. Best of all, Xerxes met the test and proved he was the man she hoped he would be in that situation. He instantly knew injustice when he saw it and acted accordingly. Indeed, her wisdom was vindicated.

The question remains for all of us: Do we each bring out the best in our spouses, as did Queen Esther in hers?

***

Points to Ponder

Marriage is a complex institution that brings together two flawed people with the singular goal to make their love for one another work for the common good of them both. That means learning to accept each other's imperfections as well as each other's strengths. Grace and humility begin in marriage when you recognize that while your spouse may be far from perfect, he or she still has redeeming qualities which deserve your acknowledgement and honor.

These characteristics are often overlooked or taken for granted in marriage, but that does not reduce your spouse's need to hear that he or she is respected and admired for what they bring to the table. It's essential for your marriage if you want it to remain vibrant and successful.

Marriage, like a good farming field, needs to be well-watered with loving attention to remain robust and fertile for growth. Such life-giving "irrigation" is made possible by the introduction of targeted surprise. Doing something different — anything positive that's unexpected, especially in the midst of marital discord — can suddenly re-channel the energies of a couple in a more constructive direction.

One husband, for example, took his wife out for an evening in which he replicated everything they did on their first date, including driving up to a viewpoint overlooking the city that in their day was called "lover's hill". He was amazed over the impact the evening had on their relationship. Three weeks later, she was still talking about it with her friends.

In another instance, just as her husband was beginning to pick an argument with her, his wife, to his complete surprise, pulled out a squirt gun and shot him with it, running off giggling. Her therapist had recommended she try this startling maneuver to break up the monotony of the nightly arguments they were having. The result was equally startling. After the third time she pulled out her squirt gun, he pulled one out of his pocket, too, and began squirting her in return. At the conclusion of their old fashioned squirt gun fight, they lay on the floor, soaking wet, and laughing uncontrollably. They realized at that moment that it was the first time they had laughed together in years. Simply doing something unexpected had jump-started a major change for them that ended up completely revitalizing their relationship.

In doing something unexpected and even risky, Esther not only succeeded in bringing to her husband's attention the dire circumstances of her people, but also generated even further respect and honor that took their marriage to a new level of commitment. Risk-taking is not usually something we talk about in marriage, but when it comes to initiating healthy change for the sake of the relationship, sometimes it's just what is needed. Marriage is often too easily "routinized" to death, and both partners are afraid to step outside of the box and try new ways to engage.

Only by breaking the rules for approaching the king did Esther discover the liberal extent of acceptance and respect Xerxes had for her. She took her chances and found a freedom she didn't realize she had before, a freedom that she used in a way that no doubt endeared her to the king. In obeying

God by doing what Mordecai had asked of her, she learned that she could shape reality rather than merely standby and passively watch events unfold to the detriment of her people.

To become more proactive in your marriage, you must practice good assertiveness skills. That means expressing your insides clearly and unapologetically and inviting your marriage partner to do the same. When someone is assertive, you don't have to guess what they're thinking or feeling. You don't feel threatened by what they've said or how they've said it. That's because there are no manipulations, no accusations, no judgmental attitudes expressed — just honest self-disclosure.

When you're passive, you don't respect yourself; you withdraw or keep silent. When you're aggressive, you don't respect the other person; you attack or belittle. When you're assertive, you're not only respecting yourself, but you're respecting the other person as well.

With passivity we see fear and retreat; with aggression we see arrogance and rebellion, but with assertiveness we see humility and service.

Whether you're aware of it or not, passivity reveals weakness to the other person, while aggression reveals merely defensiveness. It's only with assertiveness that you express authentic conviction. We are called by God to be assertive for the Kingdom, but that's only possible if we accept who God has created us to be.

Esther came to understand this when she finally realized she had been made queen to save her people. This is what inspired her to act boldly. In the process, she also discovered a new side to her that she had never before expressed. She discovered that God had created her to speak out and that demonstrating personal conviction made her more, not less, compelling to those who set the direction for her nation. What started out as a mission to free her people from Haman's decree of extermination ended up including a voyage of self-discovery.

By speaking out about her concerns with deference and respect, she drew out the best inclinations in Xerxes, who followed Cyrus the Great in exhibiting a generous spirit toward the Jews. He righted an impending injustice, and in the process honored both Mordecai and Esther as worthy of the highest praise. Despite the fact that they came from radically different religious backgrounds, together they carried forth God's program of protection for His people. Perhaps, we might call them the "odd couple" of redemptive history!

Her godly influence on King Xerxes' decision-making preserved both the sanctity of their relationship and the destiny of the Jews. As Esther learned, God has given us each the capacity to live fully, but only if we are willing to step out in faith.

That's as true for marriage as it is for any other calling.

Part Seven - Righteous Marriages

Chapter 16

Joseph and Mary: The Transparency of Kindness
Matthew 1:18-24; 2:13-23; Luke 1:26-56; 2:33-52

By now, you're no doubt familiar with the fact that Jewish marriage laws and customs were quite different than those of today. Marriages were typically arranged by the parents of the bride and groom, sometimes with and sometimes without input from the son or daughter involved. It was essentially a business transaction wherein the parents of the groom negotiated a "bride price" (*mohar*) to be paid to the bride's family for the young woman he was about to marry (Gen. 34: 12). Usually, both the bride and groom were still in their teens. In general, girls in 1st Century AD Jewish families were considered ready for marriage by age 12.

Judging from his response recorded in scripture, it appears that Joseph was clearly in love with Mary and clearly wanted the marriage. It's entirely possible that he urged the parental negotiations to begin. In any case, once the contract was agreed upon, it became immediately binding, meaning that the couple was considered as good as married, which meant it required a divorce decree to end the relationship.

That's the reason the Gospel writer Matthew referred to Joseph as Mary's "husband" even though they had yet to go through the formal nuptials. It could take up to a year in this stage of betrothal before that ceremony took place and the marriage was consummated. Obviously, betrothal was considered far more binding that we consider engagement today. In present day society, a fiancé can simply call off an engagement without fear of any legal backlash either to himself or to the partner from whom he's separating.

In Joseph's time, it was a very serious matter if a woman were to get pregnant during the betrothal period, especially if she hadn't had sexual relations with her betrothed. That was the case with Mary, and as in all cases of adultery, Jewish law called for the unfaithful partner to be stoned to death as punishment for infidelity.

When Mary confessed to him that she was pregnant, Joseph couldn't bring himself to believe her seemingly preposterous explanation and it immediately left him in a major quandary. He knew what the law said, but he still loved Mary and didn't want her punished, despite thinking she had been unfaithful to him. He must have been crushed by her disclosure. In the blink of an eye, his world had been turned upside down.

At that point, Joseph had three options for responding to his predicament, none of which was appealing. First, he could publicly charge her with infidelity in a Jewish court of law, in which case Mary could be subject to the death penalty.

A second option would be to divorce her quietly on the grounds of incompatibility, which lax Jewish divorce law allowed. All this law required was two witnesses to Joseph's statement of dissolution. To Joseph, this meant that after these witnesses signed off on their attestation to the divorce, they must be sworn to secrecy.

The third option was to formally marry her immediately so that no one would know Mary had been impregnated outside of wedlock.

The first option was simply out of the question. He couldn't stomach the thought of imperiling the life of the woman he loved, despite believing she had betrayed him. Even if she managed to escape being stoned to death, her reputation would be destroyed and her life ruined forever. That was an outcome he was unwilling to accept. He had zero desire for revenge; as far as he was concerned, it was nothing less than self-righteous posturing to play the victim in this situation.

The third option also seemed off limits, but on moral grounds. For a man trying to live an honest life, knowingly living with a woman guilty of adultery while acting as if everything was completely fine, would have made a mockery of their marriage. Such pretense was unsustainable, at least for him. He didn't want to live a lie for the rest of his life, always trying to make sure he didn't inadvertently drop a hint that their child was not really his.

After wrestling with his dilemma, he settled on the second option as the best of a bad lot; he would quietly divorce her, which, was doing the right thing according to the Law, yet also was shielding Mary from permanent shame for her indiscretion. As Matthew put it, "*Because Joseph her husband was a righteous man and did not want to expose her to public disgrace, he had in mind to divorce her quietly*" (Matt. 1: 19).

Notice that Joseph was described as righteous, which meant he wanted to do the right thing. To him, the right thing was to avoid subjecting his wife to the reproach of the community. He believed that publicly humiliating Mary was neither righteous nor humane. He believed justice would be much better served by taking care of the matter as quietly as possible.

Once he divorced her, however, others, including his family, would naturally want to know why they weren't together anymore. Everyone would also want to know where Mary had gone, since she would have had to leave town, possibly to stay with her cousin Elizabeth until after the baby was born. It's unclear how Joseph planned to handle that little detail, though he must have known that the wagging tongues of the slanderous town gossips would persist in spreading scandalous rumors. Still, it was the best idea he could come up with at the time.

Joseph went to bed that night still deeply troubled by what he felt he had to do. Just hours earlier he had been filled with optimism for the future, but after Mary's shocking news, he was a depressed and defeated young man. As he tossed and turned in his restless sleep, an angel of the Lord appeared to him in a dream, telling him not to be afraid of taking Mary home as his wife because the child within her was not conceived in sin but by the Holy Spirit. The angel told Joseph to name the child Jesus, proclaiming He would save His people from their sins (Matt. 1: 20-21).

The message of the angel in his dream must have seemed to Joseph as dumfounding as Mary's disclosure, though it probably helped him understand the exculpatory explanation Mary tried to give him. The text tells us simply that when Joseph woke up the next morning he did exactly what the angel had commanded him to do. There was no hesitation. There was no questioning what he heard the angel say. There was no further weighing of his options. There was only obedience to God's word. He went to Mary, helped her pack her things, and took her home to be his wife. That was it.

He pledged he would stand by her no matter whether others started a whisper campaign or not. He made it clear that he was more interested in

God's approval of their relationship than what the gossips thought. Mary could rest in his protection.

How relieved Mary must have felt when Joseph arrived at her door and told her about the appearance of the angel in a dream. When he apologized to her for not believing her story right away, but thought she was trying to put a good face on a bad situation, tears of joy may very well have begun to pour down her cheeks.

Just as Joseph had been having a difficult night of turmoil, she must have had a rough night of her own, thinking she had lost the man she loved and she'd have to bear the Christ Child on her own. One can only imagine the emotional reunion that must have been!

Mary had graciously understood his reaction, though his disbelief must have been a crushing blow to her. After all, she knew her story would likely come across as rather bizarre — even she found it difficult to believe at first. Like Joseph, her faith was deep enough to realize that the angel's visit was a blessing from God. To hear the Angel Gabriel's words that she had found favor with God was an astonishing affirmation of her godly character. Still, the news that she would give birth to one who was identified as "the Son of the Most High," who would ascend the throne of His forefather David and reign over a kingdom that would last forever was as dazzling as it was confusing.

When Mary reminded Gabriel she was still a virgin, the angel responded by revealing that conception would be a miraculous intervention by the Holy Spirit and the child born would be from God. Instantly, Mary replied, "May it be to me as you have said," demonstrating her unshakable faith. If God was in it, that was all she needed to know, though she probably wondered how she was going to explain it to Joseph.

The first person she turned to in sharing the news of her pregnancy was her cousin Elizabeth, whom she knew had already become miraculously pregnant in her old age and would understand what she was experiencing. She was not only welcomed, but the confirmation that it was God's doing appeared when Elizabeth exclaimed:

"As soon as the sound of your greeting reached my ears, the baby in my womb leaped for joy. Blessed is she who has believed that what the Lord has said to her will be accomplished!" (Luke 1: 44-45).

Buoyed by Elizabeth's words, Mary was ready to break the news to her husband, though she still wasn't sure how he would receive it. She knew he was a righteous man, so she likely thought he would accept it, even if he didn't entirely understand it all. But when she told him, she became greatly distressed that he found it almost impossible to believe how she became pregnant. Confused and distraught, he apparently didn't give her an answer right away, but told her to let him think how he should respond.

It was that same evening when the angel of the Lord appeared to the aggrieved Joseph. It's important to note that the angel didn't excoriate Joseph for not believing Mary's account of her pregnancy. God understood perfectly well how such an explanation would be hard to accept without hearing it from the angel of the Lord himself. After all, it's not every day that you get a communication directly from heaven.

With both of them now on board and perhaps bonded more closely together than ever before, they slowly digested the sobering reality that they were given the responsibility to raise this Child of God in preparation for His divine ministry to change the world. Their love for one another was going to be critical in providing a home where love abounded and a heart for serving others was fully nurtured, for God's very presence would be in that home.

Neither of them understood all the details entirely, but they knew that God had ordained her pregnancy and that's all they needed to know to obey His command. They clung to each other in the belief that God was in charge and that something wonderful was about to happen.

Their reactions toward one another throughout these disruptive, though marvelous events were both inherently human and deeply honest. They didn't play games with each other. They didn't pretend one thing and feel another. They both spoke from the heart with compassion and mercy, which bode extraordinarily well for the future quality of their marriage. In choosing them as the recipients of His Son, God's incomparable wisdom was on full display.

In Luke, we read that nine months later Joseph and Mary arrived in Bethlehem for the census ordered by officials of the Roman Empire, since they were of the house of David. It's noteworthy that Mary was still described as "pledged to be married" to her husband. They had legally traveled to Bethlehem as husband and wife under ancient Jewish law, but to be considered married they would have had a sexual relationship. We know, however, that Mary remained a virgin until after Jesus was born.

We are not told whether they had gone through the formal nuptials before they left to be registered for the census. The cultural environment in

Judea at the time was more tolerant of pregnancy before the actual wedding, provided that the couple was betrothed and that the bride hadn't had a sexual relationship with anyone other than her husband.

At the time of Jesus' birth, while Mary and Joseph were staying in Bethlehem in the humblest of conditions forced by the crowds of visitors registering for the census, the shepherds living out in the fields nearby had an astonishing experience. An angel had appeared in a bright light that lit up the landscape around them, announcing that in the town of David, a Savior had been born, who was Christ the Lord.

They hurried off to find Mary and Joseph and the Baby, who was lying in a manger. When they found Him, the shepherds glorified and praised God, spreading the good news of His birth to the unmistakable amazement of all who heard it. Clearly, the excitement was palpable.

Scripture parenthetically records that Mary "treasured up all these things and pondered them in her heart." In other words, she didn't completely understand everything, but still took great joy in the massive outbreak of Jewish messianic fervor. It seemed like a spontaneous revival of sorts was occurring that was re-energizing the faith of her people. To a devout woman like Mary, that, itself, was cause for celebration. She knew, as no doubt Joseph did, that they were an important part of something momentous that God was doing in their midst. It strengthened their marriage even more to be experiencing these things together.

Eight days later, Joseph and Mary presented Jesus in the Temple of Jerusalem to have him circumcised, as the Law required, and formally given his name, which the angel of the Lord had made clear was Jesus. While there, a devout man by the name of Simeon, whom God had promised he would see the Messiah before he died, approached them. Taking the child into his arms, he praised God for fulfilling His promise. Luke noted that Joseph and Mary "marveled at what was said about him" (Luke 2: 33). It was one more piece of evidence that while they knew Jesus was special– a gift from God as it were– they didn't fully comprehend the scope of His mission on earth.

Following Jesus' birth, and after the angel of the Lord had warned them, Joseph and Mary were forced to flee Judea for Egypt during the dark of night. Their escape was made necessary when King Herod had issued an edict to slay all the male children under the age of two in Bethlehem. He did this because the visiting Magi from the East, having also been warned by God, decided to return home a different way (other than through Jerusalem), thereby declining to reveal to Herod the location of the Christ Child as they had promised. Hearing that the child was believed destined to become king of the Jews, Herod was frantically trying to nip the growing rumors in the bud. No one — absolutely no one — was going to challenge his authority to rule. He had worked too hard to get where he was.

Consequently, eliminating any perceived threats to his power was all Herod really cared about. It didn't matter to him that hundreds of families were devastated in the process. It was no concern of his that the carnage he was wreaking was especially against God's people. Ironically, all of his frenzied actions were for naught. In fact, he didn't live long after that, dying only months after these events.

Shortly after Herod's death and having spent about six months in Egypt (which by now was used to receiving refugees from violence-torn countries), Joseph and Mary returned to Judea. Though they were not in Egypt for very long, they travelled a lot that year.

There's nothing like a little travel together to build a unique fund of memories that can be fondly recalled in times of reminiscence about the past. New experiences jointly encountered without the usual family or friends around tend to increase dependence on one another. Discovering the sufficiency of the relationship to sustain a sense of well-being apart from the community contributes to a bond less breakable by the storms of life. Throughout history, God had never let a crisis go to waste. Certainly the narrow escape of Joseph and Mary from Herod's clutches was no exception.

After returning to Judea, once again they were on the move. Joseph was warned in a dream that they should proceed north to the district of Galilee to remove themselves from the jurisdiction of Herod's son, Herod Archelaus. He was every bit as cruel as his father was and would likely have repeated his atrocities once he discovered that the elusive child Jesus was back in town. As a result, they left and settled in the nondescript town of Nazareth, a good place to live a relatively quiet life without being hassled by authorities.

The only other glimpse that we have of their family life was the incident when Jesus was twelve years of age and they had traveled to Jerusalem in Spring for the annual Feast of the Passover. After the festivities were over, Joseph and Mary gathered together their family and friends who had come with them, and left for home. It wasn't until they were a day out that they realized Jesus was not with them. Racing back to Jerusalem, after three days of searching, they finally found Him in the Temple courts interacting with the teachers who were astounded at His understanding of the Scriptures.

Mary gently scolded Him for making them worry concerning his whereabouts, but He asked her, *"Why were you searching for me? Didn't you know I had to be in my Father's house?"* (Luke 2:49). They didn't understand what He meant. As concerned parents, all they knew was that it was their responsibility to make sure Jesus was safe. It was just one more thing on a long list of things they undoubtedly wondered about. Joseph and Mary carried on their responsibilities in obedience to God to faithfully raise this amazing Son of theirs according to the Law and God's commandments.

When other children came along, Jesus was given more responsibility as was expected of any eldest child. Indeed, it's believed by most scholars that He delayed taking up His ministry because of His responsibility to help His mother care for His brothers and sisters after Joseph died. From everything we can gather, Joseph and Mary didn't parent like Jacob and Rachel, favoring Jesus over the others, but rather treated all their children equally.

It was their love for each other, their faithful obedience to the Law, and their shared interest in raising their children in a responsible home that made them the ideal family to entrust the privilege of nurturing God's own Son to adulthood. After her husband's death, Mary remained faithful to God's word and became an ardent follower of Jesus all the way to the cross and beyond.

Joseph and Mary left a legacy of unity forged by the challenging conditions of their betrothal, a sense of trust in God and in each other that was shaped by promise and fulfillment, and a tenacity to see things through, even if they didn't always understand what was happening or why. Joseph was a carpenter, an expert craftsman with wood and stone, who conscientiously taught Jesus all the skills of the trade. Jesus later used these experiences at Joseph's side to explain the concepts of God's generous offering of grace, which provided the foundation for the early church.

When Jesus later taught about the unity, the inherent kindness, and the gentle spirit God intended for marriage, it's not hard to imagine that He was thinking back on the relationship between His mother and father. They formed the perfect backdrop to illustrate what married life should look like.

Likewise, He taught that *"...if you know how to give good gifts to your children, how much more will your father in heaven give good gifts to those who ask him"* (Matt. 7: 11). You can almost see Him closing His eyes as He said this and remembered the good gifts His own parents had given to Him growing up.

As far as we know and whatever their faults, Joseph and Mary were exemplary marriage partners and good parents to their children; perhaps they were the healthiest examples recorded anywhere in the Bible. It's true that Jesus' brothers didn't believe in His public ministry at first and tried to dissuade Him from continuing (Mark 3: 21; John 7:3-10), but that was not because they didn't love Him. Perhaps they just didn't want Him to embarrass or endanger Himself (or the family) by stirring people up with words they thought were incendiary.

Later, when they became believers, they understood why it was so important for Jesus to go against the grain of religious authority (Acts 1: 14). They understood, too, why He was their half-brother, not their full brother, as they embraced Him as the Son of God.

Joseph and Mary were not rich in the way the world counts wealth, but they were extraordinarily rich in love, both for each other and for their God.

In the end, that's the only wealth that really counts.

***

Points to Ponder

The example of Joseph and Mary largely speaks for itself. In the beginning, Joseph could hardly have been faulted for disbelieving Mary's explanation of how she had become pregnant. After all, nothing like it had ever happened before.

It's true that among the Jews there had been a history of miraculous births here and there over the centuries. The births of Isaac (Gen.18: 10-14; 21: 1-5) Jacob (Gen. 25: 21), Joseph (Gen. 30: 22), Samson (Judges 13: 2-5; 24), Samuel (1 Sam. 1: 1-19), the Shunammite's son (2 Kings 4: 8-17), and John the Baptist (Luke 1: 1-25; 57-66) were all due to divine intervention. But these all involved natural pregnancies preceded by normal sexual relations. Each of those mothers had been barren for a long time, but God "opened their wombs" so they might bear a child.

Mary's case was demonstrably different. She had told Joseph, a righteous man who had properly abstained from sexual relations with her during their betrothal period, she was impregnated by the Holy Spirit. To the incredulous Joseph (and to any other husband who would have been told that), her explanation seemed like a pious fabrication to cover for an adulterous affair.

Because Mary had first found it difficult to believe the angel of the Lord who appeared to her, she understood how surreal it sounded. Still, she was heart-broken when Joseph drew back, signaling he was uncertain what to do going forward. He departed her that night thinking their relationship could very well come to an end, which would have left her to have the baby by herself and disgraced by the divorce. That would have been devastating to Mary.

This worst case scenario was averted when the angel of the Lord also appeared to Joseph, reassuring him that what Mary had told him was true and that he must take her as his wife, pregnancy and all. Joseph's hesitancy was likely to have aroused two competing feelings in Mary. First it would have been natural for her to be terribly disappointed to think Joseph would believe she could betray him, and that she would lie about something so important. On the other hand, as a woman devout in her faith and given the strange, unbelievable circumstances, she probably admired his piety for wanting to do the right thing.

It was never in doubt, however, that morality, not his love for her, was the issue. He was as broken-hearted as she was. Mary, no doubt, took note of the fact that even when Joseph had thought he had been betrayed, he never raised his voice in self-righteous indignation, called her a whore, nor stomped off in a rage. Instead, he was thoughtful and deliberate. There was no indication that he was anything other than kind and gentle in his response to her, which would have been attractive to Mary and a reminder of what she could lose.

In the end, this crisis so early in their marriage appeared to have strengthened their bond with one another. Perhaps this was because it completely vindicated Mary's moral rectitude, thus erasing any doubt about Joseph's implicit trust in her, and because it confirmed to Mary that she could put her full trust in the steadfastness of her husband's faith to do the right thing, once he knew all the circumstances. Joseph likely never doubted her word again, and Mary was no longer afraid to tell him the truth — a valuable lesson in mutual trust, indeed!

Joseph was a hardworking carpenter and builder who was as responsible in his career as he was in his commitment to his family. Working daily alongside His father when He was of age to do so, Jesus had the opportunity to watch Joseph deal with others outside the family, whether in business transactions or in interactions on the job. He saw his integrity and honesty in those interactions, which would have only increased His respect for His father.

Their leisure times together as father and Son, perhaps fishing together or playing a game of some sort, only cemented further in Jesus' mind the joy of spending time with him. Little wonder that in His later public ministry and teaching He resorted time and again to various analogies that reflected His time with His father.

Like the relationship between Elkanah and Hannah in the Old Testament, the marriage of Joseph and Mary in the New Testament stands out as particularly tender and sweet, highlighting a sensitivity to one another's needs and a trust in each other's love. These attributes were evident despite the hardships and adversity common to the working class Jew.

Maybe that's why that besides the miracle of God's intervention, we have become so conversant with their example of married life.

Chapter 17

Aquila and Priscilla: The Power of Lifelong Companionship
Acts 18; Romans 16:3; 1 Cor. 16:19

Rarely has a biblical couple come along whose companionship is as explicitly intertwined around both work and faith as that of Aquila and Priscilla (sometimes referred to as "Prisca" by the Apostle Paul). Their names always appear together in Scripture; they always made a living together; the early church always accepted their leadership together, and they always made their decisions to move from one city to another together.

They epitomized the insightful observation of the 19th Century American scientist and inventor Thomas Adams, who once remarked, "*As God by creation made two of one, so again by marriage, he made one of two.*" Indeed, it seems that Aquila and Priscilla had become one in all they tackled together. Along the way, it also became apparent they had mastered the art of friendship in marriage, with each willing to give more than they received.

Aquila, who had originally moved to Rome from the province of Pontus on the Black Sea, had met and married Priscilla in the city. It's not clear whether Priscilla was also a Jew or whether she was a Roman Gentile. It's also unclear whether the two of them had become Christians before or after they left Rome. Either way, Aquila's ethnicity determined their fate in the imperial city.

Though they began their marriage living in Rome, they were suddenly uprooted by an edict issued by Emperor Claudius, which mandated the expulsion of all Jews from the imperial city. This was because they were accused of persecuting their Christian neighbors. Claudius didn't really care who was at fault. He was just tired of the hassle caused by their animosity toward each other and feared that it might destabilize the smooth functioning of government in the capital. Besides, he had no fondness for the Jews, a prejudice that made it easy for him to determine whom to punish.

Leaving Rome with the other displaced Jews — the innocent as well as the guilty — Aquila and Priscilla traveled eastward, eventually deciding to settle in the city of Corinth. They were both skilled tentmakers who quickly established a thriving business there, since tents were in high demand for living and for travel (Acts 18: 3). Not every husband and wife can work together as compatibly as the like-minded Aquila and Priscilla did. They were exemplary in the way they cooperated with each other, especially in such a competitive business as tent-making. Their devoted companionship saw them through every adversity, including the normal ups and downs of work.

It wasn't long afterwards that the Apostle Paul came into Corinth looking for opportunities to spread the Gospel in the last stages of his second missionary journey. He was also a tentmaker by trade, so it's not surprising that he sought out other tentmakers in his search for gainful employment to support himself while preaching Christ in the synagogues. That's how he found Aquila and Priscilla, who immediately welcomed him into their home. They felt an almost instant affinity with the idea of working with Paul, which is why he happily joined their tent-making enterprise.

If they were not Christians before they arrived in Corinth, then it's likely that Paul was the one who led them to embrace Christ as their Redeemer. In any case, they worked tirelessly alongside the apostle establishing the increasingly sizable gathering of new believers forming a viable church in Corinth, the principal city of the Peloponnese in south-central Greece.

The city was located near the Isthmus of Corinth, the narrow stretch of land that joined the Peloponnese to the mainland of Greece. Though it was a few miles inland, it was a key commercial port city (along with the smaller town of Cenchrea on the coast of the Saronic Gulf six miles to the east), situated on the East-West trade routes between Alexandria and Rome.

It's fitting that Aquila and Priscilla, who lived and worked together, would become believers in Christ together, and grow together in their knowledge of God's Word. It served all the more to deepen their marital commitment to one another, and in ways that not even they could anticipate. From that time on, Christ's eternal love for them infused their existing love for each other to create an indissoluble bond for faithfully ministering in the early church.

Their relationship with Paul, in one form or another, lasted until his death sixteen years later. The apostle considered them indispensable to his missionary work as he went about establishing churches throughout Asia Minor and Greece, and in the end ministering in the church at Rome. Aquila and Priscilla served in the churches in Corinth, Ephesus, and Rome.

Initially, they accompanied Paul every Sabbath day to the synagogue where he preached Christ, first to the Jews and then to the Gentiles of the city. For the next year and a half, they learned the Scriptures and the fulfillment of Old Testament prophecy in Christ under the apostle's tutelage.

They had grown so much in their faith and in their zeal to teach about their risen Savior that Paul decided to take them with him to Ephesus, another port city in which he believed they could have a profound impact. So confident was he in their ability to lead that congregation that he soon left the church at Ephesus in their care to return home to Antioch, ending his second missionary journey.

Ephesus, like Corinth, was a corrupt city, filled with pagan idolatry, prostitution, and adulterous relationships. Its economy was driven by the entertainment of the constant stream of foreigners, most of whom were sailors manning the ships that arrived almost daily in port from distant cities of the Roman Empire. What better church leaders to have under these conditions than a solid, stable couple devoted to Christ and to each other. Accordingly, their ministry thrived and the church continued to grow, becoming, perhaps, the largest missionary church in the empire outside of Antioch and Jerusalem.

By studying the Word together and sharing in their ministry to both believers and unbelievers, first in Corinth and then in Ephesus, all the while running their tent-making business and taking care of things at home, their relationship continued to flourish. As busy as they were, there was always time to talk about Jesus to others who crossed their path. They never tired of sharing the Gospel, which was why Apostle Paul knew he was leaving the church at Ephesus in good hands.

It was during their time in Ephesus that they received a visit from Apollos, a devout Alexandrian Jew who was a brilliant orator steeped in the knowledge of the Old Testament. The city of Alexandria, from which he came, was considered the intellectual center of Egypt and was the most important (and largest) metropolis in the Roman Empire outside of Rome itself. It also had the reputation of having a large Christian community as well as a thriving community of Helenistic Jews.

When they heard Apollos speak, Aquila and Priscilla were impressed by his deep love of the Lord and by the accuracy of his teaching of Old Testament prophecy — except his limited understanding of Christian baptism and Christ's work on Calvary; Apollos had been told only about John's baptism and the coming of the Messiah but seemed unaware of the important particulars of Christ's ministry.

So they privately invited him into their home and tactfully instructed him about these matters so his knowledge and, his teaching could be more complete (Acts 18: 26). Apparently, Apollos eagerly soaked up this knowledge as fast as they could teach it to him.

It's safe to say that Aquila and Priscilla had a significant impact on a young man who was to be a major 1st Century player in the spread of the Gospel. In this instance and in many others, their local ministry was multiplied many times over by the godly influence they had on those who would go on to shape the contours of the early church.

They were not known so much for their ability to publicly preach the Gospel as they were for teaching others individually or in small study groups and in administering the work of the church. Their impressive grasp of Scripture and of the Apostle Paul's teaching, together with their leadership and guidance of the fledgling Christian community, left their mark on all those around them. Also while serving the Lord together as a couple, they provided living evidence of a solid marriage anchored in Christ, which must have inspired others in the church to likewise strengthen their own marriages.

To the delight of Aquila and Priscilla, Paul returned to Ephesus during his third missionary journey, remaining there for another three years and instructing the church in the Word (Acts 26: 31). That meant they had the privilege of Paul's teaching for roughly four and a half years, equivalent to a full seminary education and then some!

Such training proved to be very useful going forward. After Paul left Ephesus to retrace his steps through Greece, Macedonia, and the coastal regions of Asia Minor, Aquila and Priscilla decided to return to Rome where they started.

The church there was apparently struggling to some degree, placed as it was in the midst of the incredibly decadent, most populous city in the world; Rome was the stage on which the power politics of the Roman Empire were on full display. As was true in Ephesus, they conducted the church meetings in their own home, which became the mainstay for believers in Rome, and a safe harbor from the excesses of Roman immorality and self-indulgence.

When Paul wrote his letter to Rome from his itinerant ministry in Greece (in 57 AD), shortly after Aquila and Priscilla had settled into their new home there, he mentioned that they had "risked their own necks" to protect his life (Rom. 16: 3-5). We don't know what event he referred to, but it's entirely possible they intervened to rescue him from an angry mob, which Paul not infrequently encountered in his bold preaching in the synagogues. Among the Jewish leaders, who, consequently, were not shy about stirring up the crowds against him, Paul had the reputation of being a theologically dangerous rabble rouser.

Clearly, Aquila and Priscilla were not ones to pass on confronting a challenge. If their mentor was in trouble for some reason, there's no doubt that they would have stepped in on his behalf, even if it meant that the rioters might turn against them. As was demonstrated on several occasions, the people who were stirred up by the mob mentality didn't really know why they had assembled to start with (e.g., Acts 19: 23-41). In those situations, where all rationality was lost and confusion reigned, it became dangerous to defend anyone who was the momentary subject of their ire.

Aquila and Priscilla were movers and shakers who didn't let obstacles get in the way of accomplishing their goals or taking action when it was needed. That's why they were church leaders. People looked to them for guidance and they were not afraid to give it. When they thought Apollo, for all of his theological sophistication, was lacking in knowledge about Jesus, they didn't hesitate to draw him aside and gently instruct him on the truth.

What the people saw in Aquila and Priscilla was what they got. There were no pretentious posturings, no attitudes of superiority, and no undermining others to make themselves look better. Like the openness in their marriage, they were always candid about their mission. They were only interested in the transparency of the Gospel to all who were willing to listen and learn. They were not academics who loved to pontificate about their knowledge just to hear themselves speak. They were simple teachers who had diligently studied the Scriptures and were vocal about their love for the Savior.

About ten years later, we find that they had moved once again, this time from Rome back to the church at Ephesus (2 Tim. 4:19). The young, relatively inexperienced Timothy had just taken over leadership of the congregation there and was being instructed on how to conduct his ministry through a letter written by Paul from a prison cell in Rome. It was to be Paul's last communication before his execution by Nero around 67 AD.

Aquila and Priscilla had recently joined Timothy, presumably to help him get started on the right foot in his ministry there, since they were already well-known to the Ephesians and could easily smooth the pathway for him. Their vocal support of his leadership would have gone a long way toward winning over the confidence of the people.

Perhaps they returned to Ephesus because Paul had urged them to go there for the express purpose of assisting Timothy. On the other hand, they may have become, refugees again, escaping the persecution of Nero. In any event, they contributed significantly to the continuing success of the ministry, not only in Ephesus, but in all of Asia Minor.

The long history of Aquila and Priscilla living together, working together, and ministering together for their Lord and Savior illustrates just how powerful an impact a couple can have on those around them. Their faith was contagious, their business was thriving, and their marriage was enamoring.

They had put Christ first in their lives and it showed. Jesus said, "Seek first his kingdom and his righteousness" (Matt. 6:33), and all the things people worry about God would give to them as well. That was because He already knew what they needed. Aquila and Priscilla took these words to heart and lived them out as a couple.

Little wonder that their relationship modeled the peace that Jesus Himself promised!

***

Points to Ponder

Perhaps the marriage of Aquila and Priscilla is the best example in the early church of what happens when a couple's devotion to Christ is their first priority. Their friendship and love for one another, their generous spirit with which they conducted both their business and their ministry, and their laser focus on furthering the Gospel to a fallen world was a legacy long remembered by the leaders of the Christian community.

Lest you think that they were somehow the perfect couple, their success wasn't because they were without flaws, nor was it because they always handled everything perfectly. They weren't and they didn't. It was because the mistakes they made along the way served only to drive them more to the feet of their Savior. It was their humility toward each other and toward those they served that God honored.

Jesus himself argued that humble service is how God measures greatness in the kingdom (Luke 22: 24-27). It's not how gifted you are, or how intelligent or charismatic you are, or how you excel over others in some way, but rather how well you know who God is, who you are, and above all knowing the difference. As believers, it's recognizing that whatever success we have in life is not due to how amazing we are, so much as it is how amazing our God is who works through us. It's neither about self-rejection nor about the false humility of a superficial piety. It's about accepting God's grace toward us without trying to bargain with Him over the terms.

We have said that marriage, like any mutually dependent arrangement, is a binding covenant, an agreement two people entered on negotiated terms between equals. If either should break the conditions of the covenant to which they mutually agreed, the covenant becomes void, or at least is in danger of becoming void. We mentioned earlier that the Greek word for such an agreement is *suntheke*.

To every Greek-speaking person in the 1st Century, any kind of bond or agreement or covenant, including marriage, in which each could theoretically negotiate or propose the terms to the other was *suntheke*. These terms were often strongly shaped by cultural expectations, but normally required agreement of both parties, except where royal marriages were concerned.

In contrast, in their covenant with God, they didn't set the terms and conditions, nor could they modify or revise them, or tailor them to their ideas of right and wrong. They could only accept or reject them as given. The initiative for this covenant rested solely on the responsibility of one person (Jesus) and became actionable only after His death. Aquila's and Priscilla's inheritance of eternal life depended on it, as does ours.

Aquila and Priscilla understood the difference between these two types of covenants, which is why they never tried to alter the terms set by God. They realized that as believers their marriage was the amalgam of two separate but coexistent covenants, one conditional in that it required constant effort to keep it in good working order, and the other unconditional because it was based on God's eternal, unchangeable love.

It's important, then, to retain these distinctions if you want to understand how your marriage is a covenant and why your faith is critical to it. Marriage was always meant to facilitate worship, not to be an obstacle to it, to increase dependence on God, not to reduce it. It was intended to serve as a moral compass to the obedient heart, not to provide the occasion for stripping the heart of its tender mercies.

It was for this reason that the Apostle Paul gave his blessing to the institution of marriage as yet another means to give glory to God. Although he didn't feel his own itinerant ministry was conducive to marriage, he never discouraged any couple who wanted to marry from proceeding with their plans. He believed that every institution of the Christian community, whether it was the church, or marriage, or your place at work, served as a conduit for the message of the Gospel. He never tired of telling his listeners that preaching Christ ought to be the goal of everything we do.

The more Aquila and Priscilla learned from Paul and read the Word, the more they seemed to grasp this idea. It's what gave them every intention to make the companionship they experienced in their marriage part and parcel of their ministry to the Lord. They had learned the secret of making marriage itself a ministry.

In the process, they understood too that marriage is as much spiritual as it is physical and emotional.

Part Eight - Summing Up

Chapter 18

Epilogue: The Anatomy of a Good Marriage

We have now reviewed seventeen marriages, some good, some bad, and others in between, but all of which played a part in the unfolding of redemptive history as recorded in the pages of Scripture. We have explored them in detail to see what we could learn, either from their successes or from their failures, about the essentials to a satisfying marriage. Each couple provides important lessons in conducting our relationships in ways that can ensure the happiness we seek.

Let's summarize what we've discovered.

Abraham and Sarah

From Abraham and Sarah we learned about the general importance of *protecting your spouse* if you want your wife to feel that her safety and security and her independence are central to your concern. Sarah was never able to feel secure after Abraham showed that he was quite willing to hand her over to a foreign king if he felt his own safety was at risk.

Feeling expendable if danger lurked certainly couldn't have contributed to any trust she might have had in her husband. She was reminded again of this when she encountered Hagar's scurrilous insults. When apprised of them, Abraham calmly passed off as best left to the two women to sort out.

In today's terms, instead of shoving their spouses into the arms of someone else to protect themselves, husbands and wives are more likely to fail at safeguarding their relationship by remaining silent when their marriage partners come under attack. It could be the verbal abuse of others outside the family or it could come from within the family, such as demanding parents who relentlessly try to manipulate them. Either way, every effort that's made by the negligent spouse to rationalize the failure to intervene usually only makes it worse.

If firm boundaries are not set for your partner's protection, your spouse will inevitably feel unloved and exposed to the wolves. Divorce has occurred over this very issue more frequently than most people think, especially when it involves triangulation with over-controlling parents. For instance, if the adult child of such parents — whether it's the husband or the wife — chooses to follow their dictates over the wishes of their spouse, it often leads to angry confrontations and, if there's no change, not uncommonly to separation. Once a spouse feels it's impossible to compete with the in-laws, they often give up on the marriage altogether.

When you marry someone, you do well to remember that you are also marrying into a family. If that family is highly manipulative, or if they seem to have an inordinate amount of power over the one you're marrying, then you should prepare yourself for the likelihood of this kind of conflict.

Intrusive in-laws are not the only means by which your relationship can be sabotaged by others outside your marriage. The issue of protection is much broader than that. So, you need not stop there in finding other ways you can protect your marriage.

These ways might include, but are not limited to, spending adequate time together; making sure you don't keep secrets from your spouse; making certain that what's private between the two of you stays private; invariably speaking positively about your husband or wife when you're around others, and showing others that you won't tolerate any disrespect toward your spouse. It boils down to whether you choose to esteem your partner, both publicly and privately, or whether you choose to tear him or her down or let others do that for you.

Isaac and Rebekah

Abraham's son Isaac had the same problem as his father. He lied about his wife Rebekah, claiming that she was his sister. Like his father, he feared that the men around him might otherwise kill him in order to take the beautiful Rebekah for themselves. So much for protecting his wife, but, after they had their sons Jacob and Esau, things between them actually got worse, much worse. While Jacob favored Esau because he was a man of the field, Rebekah favored Jacob for his domestic proclivities.

As destructive to family unity as favoritism is, it not only pits children against each other and fosters their worst instincts, but also it throws the parents into a competitive struggle of their own, with each trying to win the advantage for the child of their choice. It's a game in which no one wins and everyone loses. The children become enemies of one another and the marriage of the partners becomes a subterranean, manipulative, secret-harboring, deceitful enterprise that creates resentment in every direction. Imagine how Issac felt toward Rebekah after he discovered that she had helped Jacob con him into giving him the blessing that was intended for Esau.

If marriage is a covenant between equals, then the priority of each partner must be to consider the needs of the other above their own. Parenting your children must have the same priority, regardless of whether or not you find yourself naturally drawn to one child more than another. The objective must always be to practice an even-handed *unity of purpose*. Otherwise you end up with the heartache that Isaac and Rebekah had, watching their conniving, cut-throat manipulations tear their sons apart. Their marriage was, regrettably, that much weaker for it.

Jacob and Leah

The marriage of Jacob and Leah harbored a different kind of sadness. Jacob was never in love with Leah, who was the unfortunate victim of her father Laban's dishonesty. But he was required by the circumstances to take Leah first if he wanted to take the hand of her sister Rachel, who was his true love. Essentially, that left Leah out in the cold. She desperately wanted to be loved, yet she knew she could never displace Rachel in Jacob's heart. She didn't blame Jacob. She knew the trap her father had set for him. She was simply collateral damage.

Leah did the best she could to raise her children well, though she had to settle for a loveless marriage in which she suffered intractable loneliness, knowing that her chance for emotional intimacy had permanently passed her by. While Leah had no say in the matter, it's highly unlikely she would have chosen for herself someone who didn't love her as much as she loved him. Alas, marrying for love was not an option for her.

As unhappy as it was, her experience does teach us the *importance of genuine love*, continuously nurtured and visibly cultivated in a marriage. It's the lifeblood of any marriage, which is why it must be front and center in courtship.

Infatuation and Love

In the early weeks and months of a relationship, it's important to understand the difference between infatuation and love. Both involve the excitement of romance. Both involve physical attraction. Real love means a deep attachment to the whole person, not merely to the parts you like. Love sees the imperfections perfectly, yet preemptively gives them grace. Such love has sustainability because it's not built on the quicksand of an idealized fantasy, as is the case with infatuation.

People are accustomed to thinking of love as a feeling, but that is not necessarily the case with the biblical word, *agape*. *Agape* is love because of what it does, not necessarily because of how it feels. *Agape* love is not simply an impulse generated from feelings, as infatuation is. Rather, it is an exercise of the will, a deliberate choice. That's why God can command us to love (*agape*) our enemies (Matt. 5:44). He's not commanding us to "have a good feeling" for them, but to act in a loving way toward them. Agape is related to obedience and commitment, not necessarily to feeling and emotion. It's based on behavior, which is why it is defined by what you *do or don't do* when you're displaying that kind of love (1Cor. 13: 4-7).

Dr. Barbara DeAngelis, marriage consultant and popular author on relationships, once remarked on her syndicated program that "marriage is not a noun, it's a verb. It isn't something you get. It's something you do. It's the way you love your partner every day". That pretty much captures the idea of agape love in intimate action in the life of a couple.

The Apostle Paul's writings, particularly his letter to the Corinthian church, helpfully fill in the details. The selfless nature of agape is the attitude that distinguishes it from common notions of love that are more defined by expectations than by humble service. It is action-oriented and identified more by virtuous behaviors (e.g., 1Cor. 13) than by feelings or emotions.

Agape differs from its Hebrew relative, *Hesed*, which is the term used for love in the Old Testament. *Agape* is not just a covenant love owed in loyalty to a particular person or group. It refers to a unique love defined by Jesus as a self-sacrificing love, which does not expect a reward in return, but rather is founded on grace. There is simply no quid pro quo in the world of God's love. It is a selfless love that derives its distinction mainly from its godly intentionality.

The emotional or feeling component of love, which gives love its richness and depth, is conveyed by a different term, *phileo*. When Paul spoke of "…the riches of God's grace which he *lavished* upon us" (Eph. 1: 7-8), he was making reference to the *phileo* dimension of his love for us. This second word for love focuses on affection and desire and is related to emotionally close or intimate relationships. It refers to the emotional passion and attachment connected to loving someone dear to you.

It's possible to *agape* your enemies, but it's very unlikely you'll *phileo* them. Genuine intimate love for your husband or wife must involve *both*. It's important to note that both refer to genuinely loving Jesus, therefore, both have redemptive significance.

The physical attraction in marriage is conveyed by still another Greek term, *eros*, which refers to the physical passion you feel toward your partner. It complements the other two, though it can never serve as the only foundation for a stable marriage because it tends to ebb and flow. The fact that such attraction is the primary basis for infatuation is a major reason why it would be unwise to base marriage on *eros*. It's another reason why whirlwind marriages, which are never given the opportunity to mature, are dangerous gambles at best.

No one should marry if he or she has underlying doubts about the depth or breadth of love they have for their fiancé. Family expectations, social pressure, and personal resistance to self-examination can sometimes combine to drive doubts underground, causing a person to ignore the red flags. Sooner or later, those doubts come home to roost. If that becomes the case, someone is inevitably going to end up with the "Leah problem", hungering for a love that seems to have vanished or more likely that was never really there in the first place.

Nabal and Abigail

The marriage of Nabal and Abigail, as dysfunctional as it was, teaches us still another important principle. Abigail's response to the boorish behavior of her husband, which inflamed resentments to the brink of armed conflict, was an excellent example of *taking the initiative to implement solutions to problems* rather than playing the role of the victim. Reacting proactively, yet respectfully, to a husband who wasn't easy to get along with — a man prone to arrogance and vengeance — proved to be far more effective than responding with either explosive anger or cowering fear.

Though he posed as "king of the hill", Nabal was actually quite incompetent in the way he handled people. If it hadn't been for his wealth, no one would have listened to him. On the other hand, Abigail kept things from spiraling out of control by quietly but efficiently stepping in to intervene so cooler heads could prevail. This ability was on full display in her success in calming the more passionate reaction of David and his band of armed forces when Nabal, the unreasonable tightwad that he was, refused them provisions in return for their efforts to protect his men from bandits.

Resolving incendiary situations in which your spouse is upset or angry takes tact, patience, and above all *a calm demeanor* that especially appeals to his or her need for respect. The inverse relationship between the decibel level of your voice and the credibility of your message is clearly a principle that applies here. Certainly, Abigail had learned that lesson extraordinarily well.

Boaz and Ruth

Better than almost any other relationship depicted in the Old Testament, the marriage of Boaz and Ruth underlined the importance of *selfless giving*. If marital satisfaction is really your goal, you must realize that the relationship is not all about you, it's about selflessly serving the needs of your mate.

It's imperative that you defeat the enemy of selfishness that resides within if you hope to have a happy marriage. If you honestly reflect back on most of the major fights you and your spouse have had over the years, you'll likely be forced to admit that selfish demands were at the heart of most of them. It's difficult for people in most situations to resist the tendency to look for "what's in it for me?". For the majority of us, self-centered concerns are the hardest interests to corral.

Ever notice that when people are looking for a church they often say they are looking for one that fits *their* needs, not for one in which they can most effectively serve others? In most things in life, that is our motive. Looking out for ourselves is overwhelmingly human, but it can also be destructive when it comes to marriage, which usually requires a higher level of give and take than most other relationships. It's wise to remember that life as a couple is plural, not singular.

Elkanah and Hannah

The importance of being other-centered can be seen in the relationship between Elkanah and Hannah, who added to the mix the *crucial element of empathy and compassion*. This means stepping outside of yourself long enough to understand what's going on inside your mate and, communicating that understanding back in a way that seeks confirmation. It's only when your mate feels truly heard that the emotional burden he or she is carrying is no longer a lonely enterprise, but one that's shared. This is what the Apostle Paul meant when he declared, "Bear one another's burdens and so fulfill the law of Christ" (Gal. 6:2). Happily, marriage was designed to do precisely that.

As marriage partners, we need to be sensitive enough to know when to provide empathic comfort. This is especially true when our spouses are going through hard times for one reason or another. It means being present in the marriage. When we're missing in action, especially during tough times, we're sending the message that we don't care. Contrary to popular lore, absence does not make the heart grow fonder. The excuses that you don't know what to say, or it's depressing to be around the house when your husband or wife is struggling, are no reasons for making yourself scarce during these times. Frankly, it's a thin disguise for an insufficient love.

David and Bathsheba

Providing comfort was not the issue between David and Bathsheba. They had plenty of that. Their problem was one of morality. Their relationship is the ageless reminder of the danger of wandering eyes when our present commitment has been gnawed away by careless pursuits or by too much idle time. *Personal vigilance and prayerful appeal to God's staying power* are necessary to remain faithful to His standard of moral integrity. It is pure folly to rely on willpower alone to keep our moral compass pointed in the right direction.

As David so thoroughly learned, personal reform after a betrayal of trust doesn't mean that you skirt the consequences of your actions. Sin always leaves its indelible mark. To mature in the purity of God's love and forgiveness takes a humbled, contrite heart and the willingness to set boundaries on momentary whims and desires.

Paul remarked in his first letter to the Corinthians that "no temptation has seized you except what is common to man" (1 Cor.10:13). There is nothing that is unusual about being tempted by lust. Everyone has struggled with it to varying degrees or at different times in their lives.

Indeed, Jesus himself rained on the Pharisee's parade when He commented in His Sermon on the Mount that just having lustful thoughts meant that they already had committed adultery. He was essentially telling His stunned audience that no one can self-righteously claim to be without sexual sin. Paul simply expanded this teaching to remind his readers that when they were tempted God would provide a way out so that they could withstand the temptation without falling prey to sinful indulgence (1Cor. 10:13).

When the Bible says that God will provide a way out, it doesn't mean that He will take over responsibility for your choices. It means He will open a pathway of escape, but then you must choose to take it. The best defense against sin has always been the distrust you have in your own natural inclinations. Paul is saying that to flee *from* sin is to flee *to* God, who is faithful to give us an alternative.

The most common reason we let temptation get the better of us is not because we're helpless to take precautions against it, but because we like the excitement of the forbidden fruit too much to let it go. Let's face it: Sin is enormously alluring. David knew full well that what he was doing was wrong, as indicated by all of his surreptitious cloak and dagger activities. He wanted Bathsheba at that moment regardless; it was a choice he made for which he paid a heavy price.

Without continuous fellowship with our Lord, allowing Him to guide us into moral integrity, and without any specific strategies to combat temptation, we will remain vulnerable to sexual sin. To harness temptation, one strategy to which we can all appeal is drawn from the observation that most people have deep regrets over actions they've taken that have turned their worlds upside down.

In this approach, the individual imagines that he has already succumbed to the temptation, and then as vividly as possible, reviews in his mind, step-by-step, the consequences that would ensue. These might include the humiliation of discovery, the disaffection — perhaps even divorce — of the spouse, the loss of respect from the children, the loss of friends, and so forth. Following such a review of the consequences, the question is posed about whether to proceed as planned. Keep in mind there is now a keen awareness of what the likely consequences will be. Equally important, it's coupled with the realization that these consequences haven't happened yet, and can still be prevented.

This tactic is based on the *categorical imperative* of Viktor Frankl's (1905-1997) logotherapy, which argues that you should "*live as if you were living already for the second time and if you had acted the first time as wrongly as you are about to act now.*"[5] It means intentionally considering the consequences of your questionable actions before you do them. If you're interested in keeping your regrets to a minimum, cultivating foresight is wise advice. Certainly, King David would have been better served if he had abided by such a principle.

We can see that the Apostle Paul was not arguing that God would keep us from falling to temptation without any effort of our own, without any attempt on our part to stand our moral ground. Instead, he was arguing that if we make an honest effort to resist such temptation and earnestly seek His aid in doing so, God is faithful to His promise.

He knows there is a limit to our ability to resist; there is a point beyond which we are unable to endure, which is why He knows we need His power to succeed. If we had no human ability to resist at all, there would be no sin in falling, and no requirement for His judgment. But God did not leave us empty-handed in battling temptation. It's the primary reason He created us with a sense of morality. What God created in us, He expects us to use, if for no other reason than to demonstrate our sincerity in wanting to put up a fight against sin.

It's important to remember that we have entered into a covenant, a commitment with God. God has done His part in giving us access to His redemptive power. It's up to us to do what we can to put temptations behind us by drawing from that power to deliberately make choices that please Him.

It was through his harrowing experience that David came to the understanding that the only way to deal with his guilt was to take the pathway of obedience to God's commands. His repentance was not only found in his changed life, but also in the fact that he lavished his love on the woman he'd seduced, making her and the children she bore him the center of his affection. At last, he and Bathsheba were one in mind and body, which was necessary to finally have a relationship that was pleasing to God and satisfying to himself.

Being on the same page as your wife is critical to the success of your marriage. It is, after all, a partnership. The same is true with parenting, as we learned from the absence of unity in the relationship between Isaac and

---

[5] Viktor Frankl, "Man's Search for Meaning; An Introduction to Logotherapy," Washington Square Press, 1969, p.209.

Rebekah. But what about a marriage that has all the compatibility you could ask for and is consistently faithful to God's Word, yet still ends up with a child who goes off the rails spiritually?

Hezekiah and Hephzibah

This happened to Hezekiah and Hephzibah. Their situation puts to rest the mistaken idea that parents are somehow always responsible for the spiritual dereliction of their adult children. Too many believers have labored under the unnecessary burden of false guilt_over the tragically misguided decisions their adult sons and daughters have made. It's past time for us to give them responsibility for their behavior. The Bible makes it unmistakably clear: Sorrow, even mournful distress, is appropriate, but shame and self-reproach are not.

Xerxes and Esther

When bad things happen in your life, or are about to happen, how you respond to them is of major significance to your marriage. Esther discovered this in her marriage to King Xerxes of the Persian Empire. With the fate of her people hanging in the balance, she finally found her voice in the relationship. When she spoke up, instead of incurring the king's wrath for daring to approach him without being called (which was normal court protocol), he not only listened to her request, but came to respect her all the more for making it. He was impressed that she was willing to take the risk and stick up for her people and was grateful to her for bringing to his attention Haman's heinous plot being hatched right under his nose.

It was on that day that Esther learned the importance of being assertive in her marriage to the king rather than being silently passive. She realized that nothing good would happen without her taking the risk to disclose the heavy contents of her heart directly to him. God blessed that effort, making their unique marriage a linchpin to the redemption of the Jews. More generally it should teach us all about the importance of being transparent about what is troubling us so that our spouses are no longer operating in the dark and unlikely to respond appropriately.

David and Michal

When you do speak up, if you wish to be heard and want what you say respected, then it's imperative you refrain from hitting below the belt. Both

David and Michal were guilty of this over a disagreement about his deportment during the festivities accompanying the arrival of the Ark of the Covenant in Jerusalem. She pummeled him about it the moment he walked in the door, using heavy doses of sarcasm in making her complaint known. It was not exactly an invitation to open dialog.

Likewise, he purposely hit her back where he knew it would hurt her the most. He also slammed the door to any meaningful conversation. Sadly, it was such a calamitous argument that it led to a living divorce; they remained together on the official records, but they never resumed an interactive relationship again.

The lesson from this? Learn the difference between aggression, where attack and belittling are the norm, and assertiveness, where respect and affirmation are the standard. Knowing the distinction between the two, and making every effort to be assertive, are foundational to healthy communication. Otherwise, you're more likely to fall into the same trap as David and Michal did and end up destroying your marriage like they did. It may take a longer series of such arguments than it did for them, but that's your foreseeable future if you can't understand the damage you're doing now.

Ahab and Jezebel

If you want greater evidence for this point, you need not look any further than the marriage of Ahab and Jezebel. Not only did they have little respect for the people they ruled in the northern state of Israel, but they showed precious little toward each other. The situation was made even worse by Jezebel's overwhelming dominance in the relationship.

Jezebel was often disgusted, sometimes even outright contemptuous, of her husband's weakness, both as a man and as a leader. At times she saw him as an immature petulant child, which he was. There is no doubt she ruled the roost, even though he was the king. She was disdainful of anyone who wasn't a mover and shaker like her. His frequent reluctance to take matters into his own hands earned him nothing but loathing and condescension from Jezebel. The only reason she stayed with him was that she depended on his power as king to carry out her own agenda.

The destructive criticism, the relentless churlishness, the weaponized silence —it was all there. There wasn't a shred of decency left in Jezebel, who thought nothing of having someone killed if that person got in her way. There wasn't much dignity left in Ahab either.

Their unholy alliance merely underscored the reason why, if you want even a modicum of respect, there must be at least some visible evidence of virtue in your marriage. If you're not serving the best interests of each other, but are acting out of dependency or manipulation, there is little hope that it will be a satisfying relationship. At a minimum this suggests some measure of moral integrity and personal humility. Unfortunately, Ahab and Jezebel had neither.

Hosea and Gomer

Even if virtue is missing, as was the case for Hosea's prostituting wife Gomer, the *relentless love* of just one of them — a love that transcends even betrayal — can sometimes have a redeeming effect over time. Gomer did everything she could to alienate Hosea, but in obedience to God's instructions he remained persistent in his pursuit of her until she finally recognized the futility of her own destructive behavior. Love like that in a marriage partner is rare, but when it happens it takes on a kind of missionary flavor that can sometimes conquer the hardest of hearts.

When a marriage goes off the rails and gets dragged down by infidelity, Hosea teaches us that first we must properly understand the extramarital affair (since not all affairs are the same) to determine how to appropriately respond. Knee-jerk responses are invariably unwise and can lead to regrettable interactions. Only when we know what kind of affair it was will we be in a position to determine what's required for healing, and whether it's possible to rebuild trust and intimacy.

Naturally, all of this is conditioned by the response of the offender, which can vary, depending on the cause of the affair. As we have seen, without an evident measure of remorse, repentance, and contrition, there is little chance of healing. The bottom line for both partners is this: If you want your marriage to last, you must treat it with the kindness it deserves. When it becomes badly damaged, as in the case of infidelity, your task is to determine whether such a marriage is worth saving.

Hosea concluded that despite the betrayals his marriage was still worth saving in much the same sense that God considered man worth saving, even though he had similarly betrayed Him. To Hosea, it was where faith intersected with the disillusioning ugliness of real life. As a prophet of God, he firmly believed in the redemptive power of love, even in the life of a marriage partner like Gomer.

Ahaz and Abijah

While there is only a hint of it in Hosea's marriage, there is no doubt that a marriage of unequally yoked partners existed with King Ahaz and his wife Abijah. The idolatrous Ahaz wanted little to do with the Jewish faith, even locking the doors of the Temple to worshippers of Yahweh. Abijah, on the other hand, was a faithful Jew who diligently followed the dictates of her faith. She likely grieved deeply over her husband's apostasy which was on display the moment he ascended the throne.

Their relationship gives us a glimpse of how to handle being married to an unbeliever, in this case, Ahaz, who profaned everything Abijah believed in. Like many royal wives, Abijah had no influence over the way her husband governed, but her example tells us that it is far better to *focus on what you do control*, not on what you don't control, which is good advice under any circumstances. For her it was raising her son Hezekiah to be a God-fearing man who would become the future king and determine the future direction of the nation.

In the New Testament, the Apostle Paul explained that what's under your control is your own decision to stay in the marriage, which he supported, as long as the unbelieving spouse was tolerant of the religious differences (1Cor. 7:12-14). He believed that such a marriage was potentially a conduit of God's grace in bringing that unbeliever to Christ.

Though it's doubtful that Abijah's standing with Ahaz was left unaffected by her monotheism, she probably had wished she had more clout, if only to stop the idolatrous sacrifice of their son in the fires of Molech. At least she didn't encounter difficulty having children. It was managing to raise at least one of them to adulthood that was her challenge.

Jacob and Rachel

In some ways Jacob's wife Rachel, who lived over a millennium earlier, had the opposite problem. She and her husband shared the same faith, but she struggled with the fact that she was barren. She was, at first, envious of her sister, even though she was the one who had the luxury of feeling special in the eyes of her husband. It was only later, after she started having children, that she was able to soak in Jacob's deep love for her. Fortunately for her, Jacob kept the fire of their romance alive and well until such time as she could appreciate it.

Apparently he did this by doing special things for her, treating her differently than the others, and later her children as well, things which were noticeable even to Leah, who desperately wanted the affection he gave to her sister. While Leah had babies but wanted love, Rachel had love but wanted babies. Eventually, she had both.

It's interesting how Rachel, like so many people who are "glass half-empty" types, made herself unhappy by focusing on what she didn't have instead of enjoying what she did have. It's a supreme irony that our internal narratives about events often sabotage the very joy we so ardently seek. When was the last time you reviewed in your mind all the positive attributes of your marriage instead of ruminating over everything you don't like about it? It's a fair question, one which marriage partners should ask themselves more often.

The point is that each of us is responsible for making our marriages what they are. As Drs. Les and Leslie Parrott like to put it, "Marriage doesn't make you happy; you make your marriage happy." Even over-controlling partners miss this point, largely because they're too busy trying to control the other person to realize *they* are the ones causing their own unhappiness.

Joseph and Mary

Contrary to such pessimists, Joseph fully appreciated all he had in his betrothal to Mary. In fact, it was precisely the happiness he had experienced with her that threw him into such turmoil over what to do after learning about her pregnancy. Even though he believed she had committed adultery, he still loved Mary deeply. A man of strong principle, the thought of giving her up, though he believed it necessary, was agonizing for him before the angel appeared to him. He felt there was no other choice, though he was determined to make it as easy on Mary as he could.

One can only imagine how relieved he felt when he learned that her pregnancy was of the Holy Spirit, not of another man, though it's doubtful that he fully understood it. To his credit, if God declared it, he believed it. Besides, he desperately wanted her to be innocent.

His experience with Mary revealed the importance of trusting the other person and putting God first in your marriage. Above all, it highlighted the need to *assume the best in each other* until proven otherwise. Joseph might have saved himself considerable heartache if he had believed Mary's explanation from the outset, as crazy as it sounded, and then asked God for confirmation, but his response was quintessentially human. We'd be kidding ourselves if we thought we'd have responded any differently. At least he wasn't being punitive.

Fortunately, Mary understood her story sounded irrational, and could easily have been taken as a cover for some dalliance. After all, she had a hard time believing it herself at first. At any rate, she gave him the benefit of the doubt, although she must have felt a crushing disappointment underneath.

Assuming innocence until proven guilty is a good principle to abide by in our marriages. Since we demand that of our society's system of justice, it's only consistent that we expect it in our personal relationships as well. We call trials that push predetermined narratives "kangaroo courts", despising their unfair, slanted view of the evidence. Why should we give it any more credit when it happens in the private courtroom of our marriages?

Aquila and Priscila

Assuming the best in each other is a mindset that finds its most vigorous expression in the marriage of Aquila and Priscilla. This predisposition is almost always the primary lubricant of a marriage that boasts of true companionship. Their ability to foster an environment of give and take in building, not only their relationship of love, but also their deep and abiding friendship, was crucial in enabling them to work side-by-side in both their business and their church ministry.

This is why they could move so effortlessly from one church to another and quickly establish themselves as leaders. Their invaluable contributions to the churches at Corinth, Ephesus, and Rome showcased their remarkable adaptability to different municipal cultures and different pressing needs presented by the local congregants. They proved to be quite effective in their ministry within a wide swath of early Gentile churches precisely because their own relationship with one another spoke so eloquently of what Christ's love can do in the lives of His followers.

This is what happens when you put God first in everything you do to deepen your bond in marriage.

A Final Appraisal

Distilling into bullet point form what we've learned from these key marriages described in Scripture, we can draw the following conclusions for building a happy relationship of our own:

- Practice vigilance and prayerfully appeal to God's redemptive power in your life, which is essential to any intimate relationship. Seek first His kingdom.

- Develop a unity of purpose with your spouse, one that allows for and encourages a diversity of interests and abilities based on a relentless, authentic love for one another.

- Make sure selfless giving is at the core of your relationship, which requires you to periodically assess whether selfishness has crept into your actions. Practice empathy.

- Actively cultivate a humble climate of grace, in which forgiveness for one another's mistakes is readily given and mercy is regularly practiced.

- Make every effort to *protect* your partner, which may involve setting boundaries separating those who would otherwise do your spouse harm (e.g., intrusive parents, unkind relatives, etc.). Stand up for your spouse when unfairly attacked.

- Be transparent with one another, disclosing your thoughts and feelings so that your spouse is not in the dark about what's going on inside you. Practice honesty.

- Be calmly assertive with one another, taking the initiative to propose solutions to problems rather than merely marinating in complaints. In other words, combine teamwork and mutual respect with a generous dose of admiration.

- Frame your differences in optimistic, negotiable terms rather than in the pejorative terms of disapproval. Consider your differences as strengths, not weaknesses, in the relationship. Remember, differences are the greatest impetus for interpersonal growth. They provide the continuing interest value of your marriage.

- Place your focus on what you do control, not on what you don't when trying to bring about change. That means proactively working on *yourself* rather than on your mate. Personal change, while often ignored, is the best stimulus for relationship change.

- Assume the best in each other, which includes assuming innocent until proven guilty. It's the substance of compassion and justice.

- Work on building a friendship as well as a love relationship with one another. Fulfillment is found in couples who discover true friendship in each other.

- Keep your marriage fresh by doing something different, even surprising, from time to time. Don't allow the deadness of too much predictability characterize your routines. Make married life an adventure!

As we have learned, the marriages of the Bible, both good and bad, have much to teach us about what we can do to make our own marriages the best they can be. God has not left us without plenty of models to illustrate His teaching on how to relate to one another in a way that honors Him.

Many of the things that are suggested reflect the underlying yearnings of most people for their lives, married or unmarried. In a recent survey of the thoughts occupying the minds of those who are on the cusp of dying, three regrets emerged as most prominent:

1. I wish I'd had the courage to live a life true to myself, not the life others expected of me.
2. I wish I'd had the courage to express my feelings.
3. I wish that I'd had let myself be happier.

Though we may spend a lifetime keeping it secret, what we want to feel most deeply inside ourselves is, in a nutshell, what God most intended for us to experience all along. True happiness is not so much a mystical experience as it is a metaphysical one which prompts every dream we have in life. It involves the whole person, inside and out, body, soul, mind, and spirit. When we fragment ourselves in a relationship, trying to become someone we're not, we tear at the very fabric of our humanity as God created it.

The promise of a satisfying, personally fulfilling marriage is found in the indestructible companionship of two travelers walking on the same road of life who have the same eternal destination and who jointly believe that the most joyful way to get there is in intimate fellowship with one another. Nothing else in life duplicates that feat. Nothing else better defines the social nature of such a pilgrimage.

The 19th Century poet and novelist George Eliot put it this way:

"What greater thing is there for two human souls than to feel that they are joined for life to strengthen each other in all labor, to rest on each other in all sorrow, to minister to each other in all pain, to be one with each other in silent, unspeakable memories at the moment of the last parting."[6]

A healthy marriage — spiritually, psychologically, emotionally and physically — is but another way of describing God's perfect design for discovering the happiness of companionship in the present world and for preparing us for the peace and contentment in the world to come.

---

[6] George Eliot, from "Delphi Complete Works of George Eliot" (Illustrated), Delphi Classics, Publisher, 2013, p. 5884.

About Kharis Publishing:

Kharis Publishing, an imprint of Kharis Media LLC, is a leading Christian and inspirational book publisher based in Aurora, Chicago metropolitan area, Illinois. Kharis' dual mission is to give voice to under-represented writers (including women and first-time authors) and equip orphans in developing countries with literacy tools. That is why, for each book sold, the publisher channels some of the proceeds into providing books and computers for orphanages in developing countries so that these kids may learn to read, dream, and grow. For a limited time, Kharis Publishing is accepting unsolicited queries for nonfiction (Christian, self-help, memoirs, business, health and wellness) from qualified leaders, professionals, pastors, and ministers. Learn more at:
https://kharispublishing.com/